Differences at Work

Practicing Critical Diversity Literacy

Melissa Steyn,
Scott Burnett,
and Nceba Ndzwayiba

with
Pierre Brouard,
Busi Dlamini,
Melanie Judge,
Kirsten Klopper,
Haley Mcewen,
and Jennie Tsekwa

Differences at Work

Practicing Critical Diversity Literacy

Melissa Steyn,
Scott Burnett,
and Nceba Ndzwayiba

with
Pierre Brouard,
Busi Dlamini,
Melanie Judge,
Kirsten Klopper,
Haley Mcewen,
and Jennie Tsekwa

COMMON GROUND

First published in 2021
as part of the *Diversity in Organizations, Communities &Nations* Book Imprint
doi: 10.18848/978-1-86335-238-3/CGP (Full Book)

Common Ground Research Networks
60 Hazelwood Dr.
University of Illinois Research Park
Champaign, IL
61820

Library of Congress Cataloging-in-Publication Data

Names: Steyn, Melissa E., author. | Burnett, Scott E., author. | Ndzwayiba,
  Nceba, author.
Title: Differences at work : practicing critical diversity literacy /
  Melissa E. Steyn, Scott Burnett, and Nceba Ndzwayiba.
Description: Champaign : Common Ground Research Networks, 2021. | Includes
  bibliographical references. | Summary: "This book is part of the
  movement both in South Africa and around the world to improve and deepen
  the practice of organisational transformation, and conceptual approaches
  to diversity, in ever-changing and often confusing contexts. This book
  is written as a step-by-step manual for practitioners of diversity
  within organisations, and is based on the contribution of a number of
  scholars and practitioners connected to the Wits Centre for Diversity
  Studies in Johannesburg, reflecting our advancement of critical
  diversity practice and theory, which brings the day-to-day management of
  organisations into meaningful conversation with cutting-edge social
  science"-- Provided by publisher.
Identifiers: LCCN 2021006805 (print) | LCCN 2021006806 (ebook) | ISBN
  9780949313805 (hardback) | ISBN 9781863352376 (paperback) | ISBN
  9781863352383 (adobe pdf)
Subjects: LCSH: Diversity in the workplace. | Personnel management. |
  Organizational change.
Classification: LCC HF5549.5.M5 S744 2021 (print) | LCC HF5549.5.M5
  (ebook) | DDC 658.3008--dc23
LC record available at https://lccn.loc.gov/2021006805
LC ebook record available at https://lccn.loc.gov/2021006806

Cover Photo Credit: Nicky Petrak

Table of Contents

Preface

The publication of this book is part of a broad movement reverberating around the world to improve and deepen the practice of organisational transformation and 'diversity' in ever-changing and often confusing contexts. The increasing interconnectedness of communities profoundly changes how society is imagined, making the study of the construction of and relation to our differences an area of academic priority. Though we write this book for the global context, as South Africans we believe we are positioned to contribute in unique ways. Our traumatic and divided past, as well as our complex and challenging present, offer important insights into this developing, necessary, area of inquiry.

For these and other reasons, the South African National Research Foundation created a research chair in "Critical Diversity Literacy" (CDL) in 2014, as part of the South African Research Chairs Initiative (SARCHI). The support of SARCHI has enabled the team at WiCDS to build on the lessons of our critical diversity practice to advance a theoretical project, one that brings the day-to-day management of organisations into meaningful conversation with cutting-edge social science. It also enabled us to establish a consulting arm, which implemented critical diversity interventions under the leadership of Rejane Williams, whose extensive experience and rich insights were foundational in informing the approach we have taken in this book, and to whom we are deeply grateful. We have been able to implement some truly innovative work in a number of key sectors, work that we have integrated into an ongoing research project that seeks to identify some of the key dynamics that impact on organisations learning to speak the language of difference more fluently.

As is implied in the naming of Steyn's concept of Critical Diversity Literacy, we see the process of people learning to respect and even value the differences between them as being similar to the development of a reading practice. The choice of the word 'literacy' asserts our belief that almost anybody can learn the language of critical diversity. It need not require a particular moral or political starting point; it is a capacitation, and can thus be taught. This is not to say, of course, that diversity is not a highly politicised area of investigation; indeed, in the on-going "culture wars" raging globally, differences in gender identification, and permissible speech around racial and sexual difference, are among the most divisive and partisan issues in the public sphere. To even assert as we do that gender is a social construction that has no necessary connection to biological phenotype is, undeniably, political. The notion of building the critical literacy of people who approach these subjects from traditionalist or conservative political perspectives assumes that this will ultimately affect their attitudes and that, as we explain below, a commitment to social justice is the necessary consequence of a truly critical reading practice. We make no apologies for this position. At the same time, the elaboration of specific economic or political models as part of a broader social change project is outside the scope of CDL (for the most part). We see our work here as building a vocabulary, a lexicon that helps us read the social world, and that necessarily represents only the start of a broader conversation about social change.

In this book, we hope to share what we have learned from our practical and theoretical endeavours with practitioners around the country and the world. This project has been immeasurably enriched by engagements with partners both inside and outside of the Centre, a selection of whom have contributed their valuable insights to this manual. We are so grateful to our team at WiCDS and to our external partners for their ever-critical and constructive feedback on the important work of building critical approaches to diversity. The team we introduce to you in the next section have developed their own diversity practices over years of work, and their own rich and unique approaches, which pre-date, complement, and inspire a shared practice, and even challenge it, urging improvement, greater depth, and more commitment to impact. For this reason, we present this manual as a dialogue, a conversation-starter that we hope will serve as a basis for learning and sharing in the future.

The authors,
October 2020

Profiles of Authors and Contributors

Authors

Melissa Steyn

Professor Melissa Steyn is the Director of the Wits Centre for Diversity Studies (WiCDS) and holds the DST-NRF South African Research Chair in Critical Diversity Studies. Her work engages comprehensively with intersecting hegemonic social formations. She is best known for her publications on whiteness and white identity in post-apartheid South Africa, including *Whiteness Just Isn't What it Used to Be: White Identity in a Changing South Africa* (SUNY Press, 2001) which won international acclaim, and for developing the concept of Critical Diversity Literacy (CDL).

Scott Burnett

Scott Burnett is senior lecturer in communications at the University of Gothenburg in Sweden. He is the former head of strategy at South African youth-led social change organisation, loveLife, and a frequent contributor to national debates on race, transformation and equity. Scott holds a doctorate from Wits University and a masters in social and political philosophy from the London School of Economics and Political Science. His research investigates the construction in environmentalist and land-ownership discourses of white belonging in settler colonial societies.

Nceba Ndzwayiba

Nceba Ndzwayiba is the Director of Transformation at Netcare Limited and an affiliate researcher at the Wits Centre for Diversity Studies. He is an experienced strategist in the fields of human capital development, organizational development and change, and socio-economic transformation. He was worked for a variety of local industries including the Airports Company South Africa, Parliament of the Republic of South Africa, Three Cities International Hotel Group, and the Services Sector Education and Training Authority (SETA). He is a Board Member of the Health and Welfare SETA; Chairperson of the Corporate Services Sub-Board Committee and a recipient of the Future of HR: Hall of Fame Award for 2018. He has served in a panel of the judges for Top Empowerment Awards, National Business Awards and the Top 500 Companies. He is also a guest lecturer at the University of Stellenbosch, Henley Business School, and the University of the Witwatersrand.

Contributors

Pierre Brouard

Pierre Brouard is a clinical psychologist working at the Centre for Sexualities, AIDS and Gender at the University of Pretoria. He has worked in the HIV field since the late 1980s and his current work explores the intersections of sexuality and gender, transformation and diversity. His interests include understanding the social and structural drivers of change, and the limits and opportunities provided by human rights frameworks.

Busi Dlamini

Busi Dlamini is a dialogue practitioner working on issues of race, social justice and transformation. She was part of a national rollout of a transformation process for the National Research Foundation (NRF) through the Wits Centre for Diversity Studies (WiCDS). She is a cofounding member of Democracy Works Foundation, a South African organisation working on citizen participation in deepening democracy. Busi is a 2019 Atlantic Fellow for Racial Equity (AFRE).

Melanie Judge

Professor Melanie Judge is a prominent queer and feminist activist and scholar, and adjunct associate professor in public law at the University of Cape Town. She holds a PhD in women's and gender studies, a masters in development studies, and an honours in psychology. She is author of Blackwashing Homophobia: Violence and the Politics of Race, Gender and Sexuality (Routledge) and lead editor of To Have and To Hold: The Making of Same-sex Marriage in South Africa (Fanele). Melanie is a trustee of GALA, the South African LGBTIQ archives.

Kirsten Klopper

Kirsten Klopper is an independent consultant who has spent the past 30 years working in social and economic development. Living and working in rural and township areas (pre- and post-apartheid) in South and sub-Saharan Africa, and experience with the non-government, philanthropic, public and private sectors cultivated her keen appreciation for diversity, inclusion and social justice. This led her to work as an associate of the Wits Centre for Diversity Studies, where she spent four years facilitating workshops on transformation and transformational leadership with the National Research Foundation (NRF). She currently works as a diversity and inclusion facilitator. She has a BSc (Chemistry and English), Honours in Development Studies and an MBA.

Haley McEwen

Haley McEwen is Research Coordinator at the Wits Centre for Diversity Studies, and has been part of implementing a number of diversity interventions in South African organisations. Haley's research focuses on the intersections between heteropatriarchy, white supremacy, and coloniality, especially as they operate in the context of transnational sexual politics. She was awarded her doctorate at Wits University in 2018.

Jennie Tsekwa

Jennie Tsekwa is one of the founding directors of the Kopanya Institute, a social change organisation focusing on equipping people around issues of diversity and identity. She is an experienced facilitator and coach with a passion for working with individuals and teams that are going through seasons of change, growth or stress and seeking greater alignment, connection and effectiveness. She has been working in the fields of diversity, inclusion and transformation since 2001, in the public, corporate, non-profit and education sectors.

Introduction

Our perspective on building critical approaches to diversity globally is intimately informed by the South African example. A common narrative about South Africa is that it is a great success story of conflict resolution, constructive dialogue, and the transcendence of racial enmity. The "Rainbow Nation", with its well-respected Constitution, aspires to secure the prosperity of all who live in it across lines of race, gender, sexuality, ability, and all other divisions that have historically produced inequality. The hold that this narrative has on the collective imagination is however frequently unsettled by profound discontinuities, such as the country's raging epidemic of sexual violence against women, the short and brutal lives of people living in poverty, the on-going rape and murder of trans and queer people, and a series of high-profile racial hate crimes. Our politics has become ever more robust and contentious, and our public spaces filled with increasingly angry and insistent voices clamouring for a new way of thinking society.

Our experience is of course exemplary of a historical moment characterised by changes at the global level, where war and migration, the resurgence of right-wing populism, and the growing polarisation of politics dominate the headlines. In the interpretation of certain analysts, the current crisis has been precipitated by the end of the Cold War, and the financial and environmental crises caused by the ensuing neoliberal hegemony. The particular form this moment of rupture has taken in various countries, including in South Africa, must be appropriately historicised if we are to respond to it adequately. For many observers around the world, the birth in the 1990s of the 'New' South Africa was taken as proof by neo-liberals, along with the fall of the Berlin Wall, and the Good Friday Agreement in Northern Ireland, that humanity was nearing the 'end' of history. The basic idea was that the world was moving inexorably towards liberal democracy and free markets, that this would end wars, and that human prosperity would truly be secured. What has happened since then has been very different, however. People around the world have shown themselves to be stubbornly stuck in old patterns of thinking, keeping them very much in the grip of 'history'.

Organisations are important sites for the enactment of these patterns. The news cycle of the past couple of years has left many organisations that have not been able to transform themselves ravaged and burnt out on the side of the road. Non-profit organisations have withered under scrutiny of internal cultures that enable sexual harassment; successful companies have been taken to the cleaners by staff who have experienced discrimination; schools and universities have been forcibly shut down and remodelled; while many businesses have lost customers and market share when caught out for the casual racism or sexism in their everyday way of doing business. Multinational clothing brands are punished when they launch stores using only white models, but use a Black boy when they want a model for "the coolest monkey in the jungle". Popular brands are boycotted for sexism or racism, or for instrumentalising

Black Lives Matter or #MeToo for profit. Once untouchable celebrities are publicly scrutinised on social media for the stances they take on social justice; when they are faced with serious consequences, they complain about "cancel culture". The times, it seems, are in fact changing.

The starting point of this guide is that if we are to stop re-enacting the inhumanity, dominance and oppression of the past, we will have to face ourselves and each other, and to change the way that we relate to each other as people. The 'fault' is not in our stars or even in the broad sweep of history but in the way we have been taught to understand ourselves, our entitlements and duties, and our contexts. If we are to navigate these spaces committed to a shared humanity, then a more actively engaged consciousness with what we unapologetically talk of as social justice will have to become the guiding principle for our practice.

We therefore address ourselves to people who are leading change in organisations: whether you work as a diversity consultant, a change process facilitator, a human resources manager, or whether you are a CEO, a head of an educational institution or sports organisation, or responsible for "transformation" or "diversity" at the board level or in other governance structure. We will outline the philosophies that undergird the practice, and some guidelines for implementation.

The Purpose of this Guide

Our aim in this guide is to enable people who lead diversity change initiatives to innovate new ways of applying critical approaches in their organisations. Practitioners should feel inspired to develop their own processes and tools, and to evolve the content that is shared here. Our aim is to offer the philosophical orientation for the approach: to outline the framework for the practice of building critical diversity literacy in organisations, and to allow new practices to grow from this framework.

We have gathered a multitude of articles and resources about difference, dominance and oppression, dialogue and transformation over the years. Many of these contain useful concepts and frameworks that could inform future conversations. Yet as often happens with academic work, the fruits remain relatively removed from everyday life and confined to scholarly journals and university classes. It has been part of the aim of this document to bring aspects of these sources together in accessible ways to support our own transformation work. Where these materials derive from their contexts which each have their own dimensions of difference and their own histories we have tried to extract and adapt insights and themes that might be relevant to a broad readership. To keep this guide from being too academic in style, we have opted for a less formal referencing system. When a particular source is invoked, an endnote reference will link readers to some key details about the text, with full references provided in the bibliography.

Outline of the Chapters

Making diversity *work* in an organisation is fundamentally a question of leadership. We thus spend the first chapter addressing the question of leadership. Leadership is grounded in facing up to real challenges: the challenges of an environment that has been devastated by the growth of human populations and consumption levels, of the threatened obsolescence of large swaths of the workforce through automation and other technological advances, the growing gap between rich and poor, and finally of the ever more urgent and compelling calls for true equality, for a substantively fair resource distribution for people in all their diversity, where one's life chances are not determined by societal biases.

The second chapter sketches a picture of the present. In our work with organisations we are constantly confronted with stories of avoidable pain and dysfunction: of staffroom violence, of assaults and micro-aggressions, of missed opportunities, of stayaways and resignations. It is through a close analysis of the present that we start to recognise the urgency of change. People are hurting, and organisations are suffering, because of a failure to truly engage with the social fabric that sustains them.

The third chapter historicises the present crisis. As social scientists, much of our work is focused on showing how what we think of as immutably real is in fact the result of historical contingencies, or, in plain language, of things that didn't have to be the way they currently are. Once we can understand that the world that we experience today is the result of a series of choices, ideas, actions, and accidents, and not the necessary outcome of a world that is 'naturally' just 'the way it is', we can start to make the choices, think the ideas, and take the actions that create a different reality in the future. This is the fundamental insight that undergirds our approach to social life.

In the fourth chapter, we show how theories of human diversity in the organisational context have approached their specific social visions, and how these approaches have all failed to deliver us from the particular crisis we find ourselves in at the moment. Models that "celebrate" diversity, that focus obsessively on the business case, or that understand diversity as a risk that needs to be managed, fail to significantly shift the boundaries of the social vision, and therefore fall prey to the very same social dynamics that caused diversity to be a problem in the first place.

In the fifth chapter, we introduce the notion of approaching diversity as a kind of critical reading practice what we call "critical diversity literacy," or CDL. The ten principles of CDL are grounded in critical approaches to race, gender, sexuality, class, ability, and other dimensions of difference. These approaches represent the cutting edge of academic social science. CDL is the translation of these principles into the everyday life of organisations, an operationalisation of theory into practice, and our own attempt not just to understand the world, but to change it.

The sixth chapter answers the question: Why CDL? It thus addresses the key issue for people pushing organisational change and intervention: convincing decision-makers of its importance. While it may be enough to point to the crisis that many organisations find themselves in, organisations have their own way of measuring success, such as profit, academic success, or funds raised. Approaches to diversity that see making difference work as a secondary or merely instrumental task subordinate to the overarching aim are bound to fall prey to the kinds of pitfalls we discuss in chapter 4. For this reason, we advocate for an approach that sees the diversity-literate organisation as an end in itself.

Chapter 7 moves the conversation from the Why? to the How? We present a theory of how an organisation can change: of what is wrong with the organisations we work with now, of what they could look like in future, and of how to get from A to B. We propose that what improved CDL does for an organisation is to move social relations within the organisation from *discord* to *dialogue*. This means that 'point B' is not so much an end state as a work in progress, a state of perpetual negotiation and accommodation underpinned by an ethical commitment to inclusion and fairness.

In the eighth chapter we identify the major obstacles to creating the critical diversity literate organisation: the resilient social systems that plague South Africa and other parts of the world that need to be centred in approaches to making change happen.

Chapter 9 offers some practical advice on process design and on how practitioners and managers can lead change initiatives within organisations. Chapter 10 contains some of the tools that they might find useful as part of the process to build organisations that are truly critically diversity literate.

Our Hope

We hope to be able to start, with others who see the organisation as a crucial site of intervention in creating a better world, a conversation about just how far CDL can take us to more just and equitable societies. As such, we hope that this book is used broadly, critiqued constructively, and ultimately might serve as a building block for future, and even more far-reaching work. We echo bell hooks, who wrote

> *I want there to be a place in the world where people can engage in one another's differences in a way that is redemptive, full of hope and possibility. Not this 'In order to love you, I must make you something else.' That's what domination is all about, that in order to be close to you, I must possess you, remake and recast you.* (hooks, 2009, p. 153)

Chapter 1

The Challenge to Leadership

In this chapter, we locate the conversation about diversity in a conversation about leadership. By leadership, we do not just refer to the people that sit in powerful decision-making roles in organisations. Power is everywhere within an organisation, and there are effects created by all its members and stakeholders that require a deeper look. It is not exaggerating the importance of this power to state that awakening socially conscious leadership in all parts of an organisation can create significant macro-level change.

In the first section of this chapter, we identify four global challenges to leadership presented by ecological, technological, economic, and social problems and explain why *human diversity* needs to be centred in our approaches to the future. In the next section, we sketch out a diversity-centred orientation to the subject of leadership that meets the challenges of a changing world. The final section summarises the argument.

1.1. Four Global Challenges to Leadership

Good leadership connects hope for a better future with the actions to get there, while retaining its grounding in 'reality'. It requires the ability to chart a way forward based on understanding the trends of the time: which possibilities are opening up, which are closing down. Leaders who take a narrower view of leadership may manage technically efficient organisations but may not be able to steer the organisation in a way that ensures that it remains relevant, sustainable and engaged.

If we are alert to developments globally, it is clear that there are a number of critical issues that are set to determine our collective future. Leaders need to position themselves in relation to these challenges, whether or not they are directly implicated in those sectors most responsible for finding pathways into the future on that particular issue. We are always participating, however indiscernibly, in the direction taken by humanity as a collective; history is driven by our collective orientations.

The challenge is to acquire and exercise wisdom in how we align our decisions in relation to the big challenges humanity faces. We want to be part of the solutions being sought. How do we guide our constituencies, and how can we be role models, so that we are not caught unaware by what could have been anticipated, so that we don't have to do damage control, or catch up, or attempt to unmake our legacies once history has moved on in directions we could have anticipated, but didn't? There is wisdom in reading historical tides and positioning the organisations we lead consciously and with foresight. We may pay penalties for not reading our times correctly, and leaders then carry some accountability for those consequences.

A clear example from our own context in South Africa is the leadership that steered our country into apartheid, and continued, perversely, to insist that the system continue, even when it was clear to those with a firmer grip on the unfolding spirit of the times that it was a historical inevitability that the system would fall. The apartheid leadership persisted in a national trajectory that was morally indefensible, that could never have won even sending their own children to war, many to die or to carry in their psyches the life-long scars wrought by military horrors.

Our responsibility today is to face up to the challenges in our environment that are going to exercise us as countries, as communities and organisations. These are challenges that are being flagged as needing our collective wisdom, and we are called upon take up a position, a stance in relation to what we can read in the problem. They challenge us to be mindful in our ways of being, thinking, and organizing, given the impact they may have on people's lives:

1.1.1.   Ecological Crisis

We read every day about global sustainability and the question is in the air all around us: where are we going? Global warming, destruction of the environment, the depletion of our natural resources and loss of biodiversity, food insecurity, water shortages, deforestation—a planetary crisis. The questions are big, but any leadership, in its small corner, has to think about the way it conducts business, and makes decisions that are cognisant of the consequences, of what we leave behind.

1.1.2.   Rapid Technological Change

This is a qualitative shift in technological advances—the Internet of Things, Big Data, Artificial Intelligence etc. that will bring about accelerating change, and have cumulative effects that challenge the role of humans, even the very nature of humanity. These changes, the gurus tell us, will change our reality and usher in a new era. Are we entering this revolution thoughtfully when in fact we have not yet dealt with the social consequences of the first three?

1.1.3.   Inequality

Increasingly, economists are starting to realise that inequality itself rather than absolute income level is the biggest challenge to global stability[1]. Where societies are more unequal, people are less healthy, more unhappy, and experience more crime

---

[1] This view is most famously argued by the French economist Thomas Piketty in his landmark work *Capital in the twenty-first century* (2014)

even than societies that have more poverty, but higher levels of equality[2]. As human beings, we are in many ways profoundly relational: it is not just what we have on our tables, but what our neighbours have, and the power relations that sustain these dynamics, that influence our wellbeing. Even as millions of people have been lifted out of technical poverty worldwide, inequality has persisted both within nation states and transnationally creating the conditions for mass migrations, military conflicts and popular uprisings.

1.1.4. Diversity

This is the fourth and final major challenge to leadership. Globally, societies are increasingly characterized by heterogeneity, and are continuing to change in ways that challenge us to take on the project of "being different together"[3]. We are currently living through a massive acceleration in the advancement of communication, technology, transport, commodification, financial transactions, migration, the flows of ideas, of wealth and of poverty. People and societies are changing accordingly. While there is some convergence and flattening of differences across the globe along with these transnational flows, in reality more nuanced, complex combinations of differences are being produced all the time.

This is not however such a new thing. All societies have always been a home to diversity. Throughout modern history, however, difference has been "managed" though oppression, through trying to make it invisible, through exclusion or insisting that those who are not part of the dominant norm have to conform. The successes of movements such as the civil rights movement in the United States, the anti-apartheid movement in South Africa, the Māori protest movement for indigenous rights in Aotearoa/New Zealand, and various social moments such as the feminist, disability, and LGBTI identity movements, have championed the rights and interests of oppressed and marginalized people, in a decolonial and liberatory direction. So difference has in fact always been there; and it is because of liberation and expanding human rights that it now seems to be more present, more visible, and recognized.

1.2. Our Leadership Orientation

Our approach to leading in the context of this challenge is that it is unrealistic and counter-productive to try to put the lid back on difference. The fact is not simply that we have to talk about our differences, but furthermore that we must have the *language* and the *skills* to talk with each other in constructive ways. And this can be tough!

---

[2] This argument is spelled out in very accessible form by Richard Wilkinson and Kate Pickett in their book *The Spirit Level: Why more equal societies almost always do better* (2009).
[3] This was the name of a key book on diversity interventions studied by postgraduate students at the University of Cape Town, and edited by Melissa Steyn (2010).

For many people, the acknowledgement that our societies are still deeply divided along racial, economic, gender, and colonial lines is a painful one to make but for those from historically oppressed positions it may be experienced as an opportunity to finally breathe. Some people, especially those with vested interests in the status quo, may resort to destructive ways of coping, enacting resistance, or denial. These reactions seek to close down the space for conversations. Sometimes the fact that positive change has happened in the past becomes a reason to stop talking: "we have spoken enough, it's time for less talk and more action!" or "they will never be happy with how much progress has actually been made!"

The problem with this view is that it denies our present wounds and ignores on-going injustices, overestimating our competence to enact meaningful change. It is our position that the less we talk about these issues the more powerfully and unpredictably they will continue to affect us in the future. There is no benefit in trying to deny that each of us, in one sense or another, is an indirect or direct victim or beneficiary (often a mixture of both) of racism, sexism, ableism, heterosexism, and various other hierarchical chauvinisms. In terms of race, the fact of racialisation wasn't miraculously erased by the Civil Rights movement, nor by the swearing into office of Nelson Mandela; the children born into these contexts since then have not been lucky enough not to be affected by a racialised society. Problematizing the status quo and working to build the kind of future we want to see, requires critical introspection and awareness that does not shy away from owning complicity in structures of oppression.

This means a difficult realisation for leadership: leaders can't simply "be oneself" and let the past take care of itself. So much of popular culture valorises being "true" to yourself and your beliefs, or standing up for your opinions, or feeling *entitled* to an unpopular opinion. But this is a rather shallow approach to our own humanity. We may indeed be entitled to our beliefs but participating in society means that we owe it to each other to *examine* them, and to be open to changing our minds, largely because our beliefs often have deep consequences for the people around us. Critical diversity literacy will frequently ask leaders to stop, take a step back, and start to question some of their most passionately held opinions. And this can be an unnerving and even scary process for many people.

So this is a difficult thing to do, but it also may end up being one of our most enduring contributions to a more humane world. We need to sharpen (rather than diminish) our awareness of inequalities and the unwritten rules that keep them in place. When we see that some are marginalised and excluded for the benefit of others, we have to question more often and more persistently, rather than backing off, leaving be, and keeping the peace. We need to learn more about (rather than ignore) the intricate psycho-social workings of racism and other forms of oppression.

This process does not necessarily have a static end-goal. Sometimes, use of words like "inclusion" or "transformation" suggests this: that we have a clear pre-imagined utopia in mind, that something will be transformed from state A into state B. Of course, we all hope that the future will be better. But our leadership orientation is to always see people and organisations as works in progress, as learning through interactions with others. Transformation is therefore a process that is never finished. As human beings, we are learning continuously, and organisations adapt and grow. We do not reach an end state where we can say that there is no transformation left to be done.

While it might not have a singular end-state, transformation is also not morally or politically neutral. It identifies, problematises, and historicises power inequalities in the present, and unapologetically advocates for their removal. It is at the least an ethics of distribution: unequal distributions are assumed to be unfair distributions unless proven otherwise. It is not useful or desirable to shy away from issues of power and ownership and agency and belonging. Our intuitive senses of people's entitlements might not hold up once we start to unpack how injustice has played a role in determining them. Most modern-day societies bear the marks of some form of colonial undertaking, which affected nearly all of the earth's land mass, and part of addressing this must be an openness to decolonising our thinking, our customs, and our institutions. These are deeply political and ethical but also highly complex and uncertain undertakings. The end point of transformation is not a scientifically available truth: it is a process where every actor has a claim on steering the conversation. When we approach the process uncritically, it can easily be misused or hijacked, even unconsciously, to reinforce dominant agendas and protect hierarchies.

1.3. Ethical Leadership at all Levels

Equally important to remember is that 'leadership' is distributed throughout an organisation and not a matter solely for board members and executives to think about. The process of forming leaders is a complex societal one that starts in our experiences of social roles long before we even join organisational life[4]. At every point in the "leadership pipeline"[5] whether managing yourself, others, functions, or the enterprise as a whole there is always room to position diversity as a strategic imperative. While higher management levels may set the tone of organizational culture, it remains determined at the individual level by all members of an organisation, whose self-management and personal transformation constitute how diversity is experienced by stakeholders. Our approach to meeting each other in our difference is going to be profoundly shaped by life experiences, and the ethical frames we bring from our homes and communities. Building ethical leadership can be thought of as making room for a willingness to engage with difference and also with difficulties. There are six kinds of *willingness* which are salient to discuss here. The first is a *willingness to*

---

[4] Nkomo, Stella M., and Drikus Kriek. 'Leading Organizational Change in the "New" South Africa'. *Journal of Occupational and Organizational Psychology* 84, no. 3 (1 September 2011): 453–70. https://doi.org/10.1111/j.2044-8325.2011.02020.x
[5] See Charan, Drotter and Noel (2011).

engage with the historical moment. The conditions for mutually respectful human relations built on equality can never be dislocated from the context of time and place. They are not general, ahistorical, acontextual abstractions, but profoundly caught up in the messiness of real life. The second sees ethical leadership in a diverse society as closely linked to a *willingness to engage in self-reflexivity.* This goes far beyond a "respect for differences" and includes educating ourselves in "reading" the way people are positioned in relation to each other within particular social arrangements, how they speak from these different positionings, acknowledging privileges and oppressions and how they intersect and bolster each other. This self-reflexivity should prevent us from denying, minimizing, or defending unequal social orders. It includes the willingness to ask hard questions: Who is silenced? Who is left out? Who feels most comfortable? Whose interests are served by the current arrangements? It requires respect for the individual, but in a "thick" way—not expecting people to leave large parts of who they are at home because of pressure to assimilate to a dominant culture, but rather respecting also the fullness of how history shaped them, how social and cultural influences work through their lives. It means a willingness to engage with these positionings in such a way as to create enabling possibilities for greater equality, for a greater number of people.

Ethical leadership requires more than just living in the flow of easy, unproblematised "common sense" which is really just the "normalization" or "naturalization" of dominant prior and current power relations that have become everyday. Here we are talking about the *willingness to recognise ideology at work* as it tries to convince us that the task at hand is just to reproduce the status quo; that indeed not to do so is dangerous. Two other kinds of willingness flow from this point. The first is that when we refuse to submit to the way things are, we (re)connect with a sense of the harms done, and express a *willingness to feel outrage.* Ethical choice is intolerant of injustice. Unethical leadership is complacent with inequality in our spheres of influence; it is willing to participate in, or worse, to obscure inequity, it ridicules transformation, it takes benefits that can accrue on one axis of difference, and does not conscientise itself on the ways other differences may be disadvantaged by that benefit. The other consequence is a *willingness to make hope evident* in the way we think about things, in how we talk and behave. This is not childish idealism: we can and do make progress on social issues, even as every new era brings new challenges to the gains, new evils to be defeated. Steadily, we can keep the energy cooking for a better life for more and more people, the hope that we will live together well. Ethical leadership does have an inspirational role.

Finally, ethical leadership requires the *willingness to remain vigilant,* alive to how power reconfigures, piggy backs on new prospects, co-opts other possibilities, incorporates resistances, disguises itself and passes itself off as something other than it is. The ways in which power relations intersect to reinforce, qualify and contradict each other can be confusing, especially in times of social transformation when things are so much in flux. The touchstone for ethical leadership in relation to equity is to listen through the "noise," to look through the smoke/fog thrown up as people jostle to promote their own interests, and to stay true to the historical task. We must stay attuned to what we need to put right, a task which is far from completed, and act in ways that are possible, each in our own sphere of influence.

1.4.   Conclusion

Leadership in the present applies to all people involved in social life, not just those at the helms of their organisations, although the pressure on these figures can be great. Ecological degradation, a changing technological landscape, a growing gap between the haves and the have-nots, and accelerating calls for full and true inclusion of the full diversity of humanity in organisational life are the major challenges facing leadership today. In order to meet these challenges, leadership at all levels of organisations and at all stages of development must become more engaged and take greater risks. These risks include understanding that ethical leadership means being willing to engage with the historical moment, to be self-reflexive, to challenge the common sense of the status quo, to connect with our outrage as well as our hope, and to always remain vigilant. A propensity for creatively thinking outside of established orthodoxies and received wisdoms is crucial not just for the future of specific organisations, but for all of humanity.

Chapter 2

The Organisation in Crisis

Around the world, the cases of organisations tearing themselves apart from the inside are mounting up. With every news cycle, the unfair practices of a university or a school, the racist adverts of a business, or the sexism of a charity are exposed, whether on social media or through traditional channels. Sometimes, this exposure has salutary effects: visionary leaders step in, aggrieved parties are listened to constructively, and positive changes are made. All too often, however, public scrutiny is met with denial and deflection. Leadership retreats into a pattern of recrimination and punishment, blaming the victims of discrimination, or a hostile public, or a convenient scapegoat, as being the source of the problem. The sheer recurrence of these crises should be proof enough that the problem is systemic, and even epochal: all the wiring of the organisation, its assumptions and its practices, must change if it is to survive the historical moment. Too few leaders recognise this.

In this chapter, we first describe the nature of the current crisis, and argue that part of the problem is the weakness of the project of 'diversity management'. As it is useful to identify the symptoms before making a diagnosis, in the third section we offer a portrait of what an organisation in crisis looks like. We argue that the fact these symptoms are so generalised across a number of organisations in all sectors is evidence of a systemic problem. The final section offers a brief summary of the argument.

2.1.   A Moment of 'Disjuncture'

The current state of affairs is clearly unsustainable. A broad variety of organisations, from large corporations, to universities, to international aid agencies, are host to calcified and old ways of thinking, even as the social norms around them have shifted. Too many organisations still harbour fossilized ways of thinking and risk going extinct because of it. In the twenty-first century, surviving means developing symbiosis with your stakeholders not destroying your social or ecological environment cultivating relationships with people on terms of equality and partnership, rather than on hierarchies of power and coercion.

The current moment has brought with it what may seem like a plethora of 'new' identity demands: gender identities that were not taken into account before, entitlements for disabled people that seemed unattainable until just recently, assertions of rights to free public goods and other kinds of access that shock people who were raised under a different dispensation and ideology. In South Africa and elsewhere, newspapers, radio talk shows, and social media are filled with the latest examples of just how badly we are failing to sustain organisations through the spirit of partnership and dialogue:

- Respected high schools squander the goodwill of their own communities when it is revealed that they implement hair and uniform regulations in ways that unfairly target and marginalise learners on racial grounds.

- Trusted non-profit organisations and charities are shown failing to deal with sexual harassment and gendered forms of coercion and violence, and are severely affected both in terms of funding and the partnerships they need to implement programmes when it is shown that their own management of power, of inequality, of injustice inside the organisation is at absolute odds with their purported mission.

- Powerful global fashion brands try to enter the new markets such as South Africa with marketing campaigns that reproduce the desired racial national profile of apartheid, losing customers and facing international condemnation.

- Once untouchable entertainment industry figures protected by the patronage networks of powerful patriarchal structures are exposed as serial abusers, sexual harassers, and rapists, while their enablers are publicly pilloried and rightly bankrupted.

- Multinational accountancy and audit firms, state-owned companies, public relations agencies, and even political movements are 'captured' by forces that exploit anger at inequalities to undermine the rule of law in the interests of a parasitic elite.

- Students look at their universities and say: they haven't transformed, we feel stuck in an exclusionary and elitist space, we don't feel at home here, we feel that this curriculum reproduces colonial relationships, we don't see commitment to practices that are transforming the culture of the institution.

- Attempts to force change in deadly police states see neighbourhoods transformed into warzones; activists and members of the public are teargassed and shot with rubber bullets by police; violence escalates and causes serious injuries and further deaths.

The great moment of crisis we now find ourselves in is also what some political theorists[6] would call a 'conjuncture': a moment where a number of social forces come together to upend the established order and install in its place a new one. What this means is that despite the doom and gloom of some of the prognostications our current moment is also an opportunity to forge a new sense of solidarity between stakeholders in society. Essential to the notion of conjuncture is the idea that we can find new ways of making sense of ourselves and our place in the world. In this understanding, our own identities shift to the extent that we are able to articulate them in how we communicate. New ways of *thinking* about labour, community life, environmental protection; new ways of being politicians, businesspeople, activists; new institutions that see our schools, universities, social change organisations, and even families transformed. This book is part of the project of making sense of a new and better way to live our lives in organisations, one that both makes sense and that makes the world a better place.

2.2.   The Stalled Project of 'Transformation'

The internal dynamics visible within organisations are continuous between organisations and across a variety of social groupings. From schools and universities, sports teams and civil society organisations, to small businesses and large multinationals, organisations are grappling with the impossibility of insulating themselves from society in general. Looking at the specific symptoms of organisations in crisis is a good way of starting to get to grips with why building critical diversity literacy is one of the essential challenges of our age.

Here, we will rely on a description of some of the dynamics in South Africa, which is both a paradigm case of the establishment of the post-Cold War neo-liberal world order, and a unique instantiation of a particularly violent racial order. After the transition to a democratic system in the nineties, South Africa was supposed to implement radical policies to make sure that wealth and power were transferred from the white minority (with its heteropatriarchal structure) to the Black majority (in a generally more equitable society along all Constitutional dimensions). For changing the workplace, policies such as Employment Equity (E.E.) and Black Economic Empowerment (B.E.E.) were introduced under the general moniker of 'transformation'. Now, nearly 25 years after the promulgation of the legislation that called for transformation, one would expect that organisations had made some progress.

This is unfortunately not the case. A depressing picture of the state of 'transformation' is offered by the Commission for Employment Equity's annual

---

[6] Most notably the French Marxist Louis Althusser (1967) and the 'post'-Marxists, Ernesto Laclau and Chantal Mouffe (1985/2001).

reports[7] on the distribution of positions within organisations in South Africa by race, gender, disability, and other factors. Top management positions remain disproportionately occupied by able-bodied white men, to an overwhelming degree even. When organised by race group, it is clear from the data that South Africa has hardly dented its apartheid-era inequities in leadership positions. Apartheid has survived and even prospered at the level of a trend in the vast majority of South African organisations, not directly falling under government.

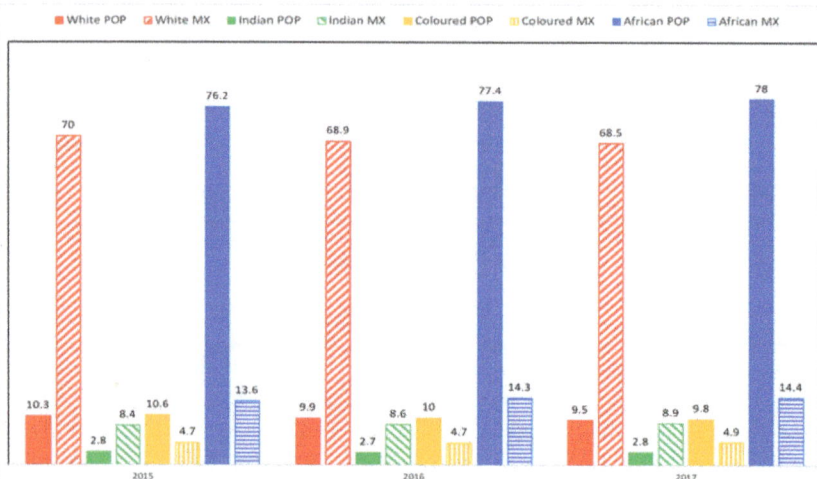

Figure 1: Top management positions in South Africa by race group, comparing 2015, 2016, and 2017

One positive characteristic of the South African approach is that progress against apartheid-era race groups is tracked by a variety of agencies and non-profits. It might seem jarring to international readers to see the categories Black, White, Indian, and 'Coloured' reproduced so starkly, but as these four groups were subjected to a racial hierarchy under apartheid, measuring progress in dissolving that hierarchy requires keeping track of these terms. And the results are startling. In the graph below, 'POP' refers to the percentage a race group makes up of the Employment Active Population (EAP) basically, people between the ages of 15 and 64 years old who are either already employed who are looking for work. This figure gives a fair sense of how many people *ought* to be represented in each layer of management if the distribution was completely aligned with the actual population of the country. The 'MX' figure

---

[7] The Commission for Employment Equity report is published on the Department of Labour's website (www.labour.gov.za) every year. These graphs have been compiled from the reports from the available reports from the last 3 years (Commission for Employment Equity, 2015, 2016, 2017).

given refers to the proportion of the top managers (from all sectors of society, including private, public, and non-profit) who are in that population group.

What this graph reveals is that whereas Black people have been steadily increasing as a proportion of the EAP, they have not had similarly large increases in their proportion of Top Management, and are still extremely underrepresented. White people are very much over-represented in top management; Indian people are slightly overrepresented and Coloured people are very underrepresented.

The organisational culture of these organisations is likely to be driven by a very white and also a very male way of looking at the world. In Figure 2 you can see the progression over three years for gender, where the EAP ('POP') is compared to positions in Top Management.

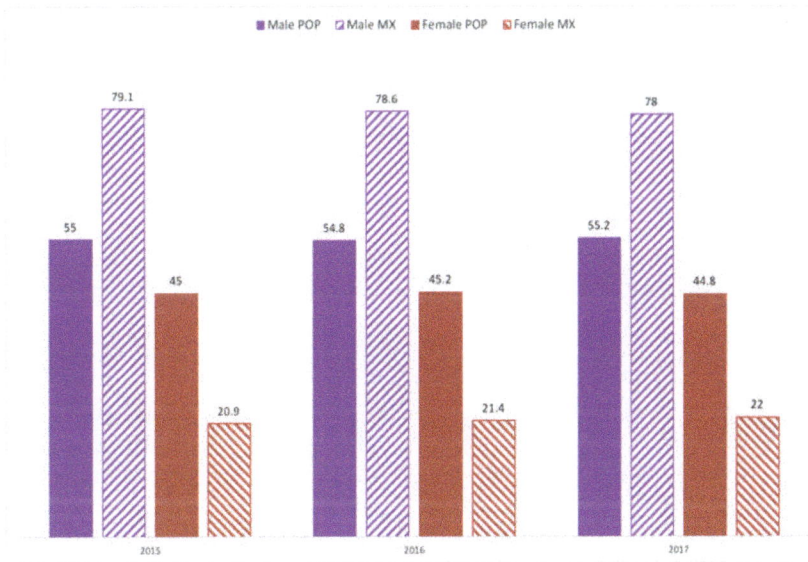

Figure 2: Top management positions in South Africa by gender, comparing 2015, 2016, and 2017

If you combine the race and gender figures, a alarming figure pops out: white men, who are less than 5% of the EAP, make up over half (50.8%) of top managers across all sectors in 2017. The situation is worst in the private sector. People with disabilities made up only 1.2% of top management positions in 2017 despite estimates by

Statistics South Africa that 7.5% of the South African population has a disability of some kind[8].

Much of this book relies on theories about the social construction of difference, which relies on research that is qualitative and often critical of 'positivistic' or 'scientistic' approaches to human social life. Quantification and statistical measurement is however crucially important. In the South African example, tracking the gender, ability, and race group of people in organisations is a crucial tool for measuring progress (or more accurately, lack of progress) towards equity goals. These numerical targets are of course not the end of the story. Transformation is more than just about getting Black, female, trans, or queer people into institutions: it is also about what those people are allowed to do, and what they represent symbolically in that organisation. In addition to the numbers, we must analyse how the experience of inequality plays out in what it feels like to work in these organisations. Even 'good' numbers can sometimes mask a damaging underlying reality.

2.3. A Portrait of the Organisation Tipping into Crisis

People are hungry for justice. They're hungry to be recognised, and to be seen, and to be acknowledged. And they want fairness. People know what is unjust and unfair, and where power is being misused and abused. They may not have a language for it yet, but they know it and recognise it…

– Kirsten Klopper

The bad news is that many organisations both in South Africa and around the world today are tinderboxes of discontent and frustration. The good news is that a growing number of people want this to change and often express a willingness to be part of positive change themselves. As diversity practitioners, we are often frustrated by being called in at the last moment to deal with situations only when things have already become very bad. This, despite the fact that there are always warning signs within an organisation, that might have been managed in advance. Once the crisis has arrived, dealing with it distracts leadership from implementing more systemic and lasting change. The problem is not likely to be just in one place one set of attitudes, one policy, or a problematic team member. It is more likely to be deep in the social systems of the organisation. It makes much more sense to manage these systemic issues proactively, before they boil over.

What we have noticed in our years of practice is that the characteristics of the organisation that is tipping into crisis seem to fit to a particular pattern a way of

---

[8] See the Stats SA special report on persons with disabilities that was compiled in 2014 based on analysis of national census data (Statistics South Africa & Lehohla, 2014).

describing what it is like to work there that speaks across various types of organisation to a deeper systematic problem underlying the events in their context. It is important that people who are interested in creating positive change in organisations are able to spot the problem signs, and to implement deep-ranging and lasting changes in the organisation, to prevent a full-scale crisis from setting in. Here, we offer five broad sets of symptoms you need to look out for.

2.3.1. The Ostrich: "Heads in the Sand"

An organisation that pretends that society and its problems stop at its doors, and that they have somehow escaped the trends of racism, sexism, homophobia, classism, and ableism, has its head firmly stuck in the sand. It is impossible for any organisation to exempt themselves from broader societal processes. In fact, a claim that specific problems do not exist in the organisation is more often than not an attempt at denial: a sweeping under the carpet of the experiences of people who do in fact find themselves in marginalised social positions.

But even with the best intentions, people may say things like *"I don't see you as Black, I see you as a person"* or *"We don't have many gay people working here so it is really not an issue for us"* and thus create the illusion that racial difference, or sexual diversity, are not daily realities for their stakeholders. *Not seeing* is not that different from *erasing*. If discrimination is experienced as racial, but asserted not to be about colour, and deflected to competence, team members can feel as if their experiences, and indeed their very existence, are being erased. It clearly needs to be spoken about, and not swept under the carpet.

Many people join the world of work thanks to members of their community who have sacrificed much to see them succeed. They have done so against personal and societal odds. When colleagues expect team members to be silent about aspects of their identity, because they consider them irrelevant to their professional lives, this is also a refusal to see people for who they feel themselves to be, a refusal to acknowledge them. This is before one even starts to consider the deep structural ways in which these aspects of our identity have affected all of our progression, and performance.

There is also an oft-repeated pattern of people in powerful social positions abrogating to themselves the right to adjudicate whether or not discrimination was or was not unfairly linked to race/sex/disability/etc. based on whether the person doing the discriminating *intended* to do so. A key theme of this book is that intentions are slippery things: our own intentions are not always transparent to us, and we can easily obscure them behind face-saving denial. Even with intentions we think of as 'good', we can reproduce racist or sexist structures. The point is that the person who has been on the receiving end of treatment they perceive as unfair deserves to be listened to and believed. To refuse to listen to stick your head back in the sand is to assume the position of the ostrich.

2.3.2.   The Peacock: "Keeping Up Appearances"

For some organisations, their reputation with customers is the only guiding principle they have: image is everything, and they have to keep up appearances. To these organisations, the public relations fallout from a racist advert is the only reason not to be racist in the first place. If they decided that their consumer base was sufficiently bigoted, it would not be a problem for them. All morality is thereby subjugated to brand value.

More equality, more organisational justice, is often viewed positively by customers. In the South African context, it is possible to observe many instances where brands build the outward appearance of having 'transformed'. This is often however mere 'window dressing': using African languages in their names, Black faces in their advertisements, or appointing a Black executive or Board member in a portfolio specifically linked to government or other stakeholder relations. Schools will avoid the appearance of being whites-only, and admit enough wealthy Black learners or provide just enough scholarships to provide a credible picture of integration in their marketing material. At heart, they will often remain untransformed, white spaces.

Some organisations will start to take their employment equity reports a bit more seriously, and see their ability to attract government business, or a broader customer base, as a good reason to present a more transformed profile. If change is only driven to achieve a target, and not for any reason connected to the ethical values of the organisation, the designated groups who are brought in "for the numbers" are treated in a default dehumanising and exclusionary fashion[9] that avoids any engagement with what an empowering organisational environment might look or feel like. When transformation targets are seen as an externally-imposed inconvenience, the strategy that emerges is much like the story of Noah's Ark[10] in that it involves bringing on board "a pair of each kind" with no account of what happens thereafter. This shallow approach to diversity fails to transform the prevailing assimilationist Eurocentric culture in corporations and fails to tackle power dynamics and inequality.

> *Organisations may be performing reasonably OK in terms of their scorecard but the fundamental relationships don't shift... We'll make sure that 2% of our employees are disabled, for example, but not do the work of really including them. Diversity is being invited to the dance; inclusion is when you're actually dancing. It's not just a rearranging of the deckchairs, where essentially the same people remain marginalised. It's like, with race: add Black, mix and stir. It doesn't fundamentally shift things. Social institutions,*

---

[9] See Selby and Sutherland (2006) for a discussion of the do's and don'ts of "making space" for people in an organization.

[10] This characterisation comes from the American scholar Laura Liswood's book, *The Loudest Duck: Moving beyond diversity while embracing differences to achieve success at work* (2010).

the way that society is structured, serve to reinforce harmful social systems, and then deliver this mixed message about diversity you're welcome here, but you're not equal: some are more equal than others.

– Kirsten Klopper

Exclusionism and tokenism can be intimately linked in the way that people describe the experience of working in these spaces. Organisations that bring in people simply as tokens of what makes them different, in order to extract the value of their difference, whether for the sake of appearances or to win a government contract, are peacock organisations: all display, and no substance. These organisations may extract market insights from say, Black employees, in ways that treat them not as valued team members and co-creators of value, but as informants. Black people make up the bulk of the market in South Africa, and yet very few of the private enterprises making money off this market are led by Black people. The same could be said of women being cornered into saying 'what women want' or homosexuals who are hired to capture their 'pink' rand, dollar, or shilling. A related dynamic treats difference as a set of known and pre-determined characteristics, so that hiring a woman brings a 'feminine' touch to a workplace, or gays give your marketing campaign a more 'edgy' feel.

Exploiting difference means that environments don't change. This can be unpleasant for employees; it can also be dangerous:

One company went on a drive to hire women miners to work underground. Safety measures in general were seen as being too costly by management and got put on the back-burner. The women needed overalls that would actually fit their bodies, but they got the same as men, which didn't fit. This is a major safety hazard. People could get injured and die underground!

– Haley McEwen

Organisations that manage crises of difference and the diverse identities of their stakeholders and staff, as opportunities to enhance their external appearance are ultimately treating people as means to an end, and not as ends in themselves. What appears to be glossy and attractive on the outside the display of the peacock's feathers turns out on closer inspection to be a mess of contradictions and bad experiences on the inside. The other side of the peacock coin is thus the beast that is "ugly on the inside" which we discuss in the next section.

2.3.3. The Beast: "Ugly on the Inside"

There are a variety of ways to describe what it feels like to be part of an organisation that is "ugly on the inside": we have already encountered above the feelings of erasure, of exclusion, of being merely a means to some other end. What brings these descriptions together is very often the notion of a "corporate culture" that people who join the organisation are confronted with and urged to sign up to.

Organisations will very often pride themselves on their internal culture, whether it's a formal set of precepts and symbols, or a more intangible "smell of the place"[11] that governs everything from innovation to efficiency. The point is not of course that organisations should not pay attention to their internal culture, but that the experiences of people within their institution of this culture are often strongly divergent. One reason for this is that people who defined the culture in the first place, (usually men, and in many cases white, given the history of vast swathes of the planet) tended to be quite homogenous. More often than not, these people are insensitive to that homogeneity: for them, it is just the way the world is, and they are not challenged to consider the extent to which their assumptions about the world are filtered through raced and gendered power structures.

Learning to play by these rules, and fitting the mould of the expected body not being too feminine if you're a woman manager, playing straight if you're gay, or fitting in with the white crowd if you're Black often builds in the people who get it 'right' an immense sense of achievement and pride. You're an executive now: you've mastered the model. In some cases, these people become the most dutiful enforcers of the monolithic corporate culture.

In other cases, however, the assimilation is unsuccessful. People try to fit in with the dominant culture, but never fully feel at home. This is experienced in profoundly emotional terms by team members:

> *People experience feelings of not being taken seriously, feelings of anger, feelings of hurt, feelings of exclusion, feelings of coming into an institution which just has no place for them.*

> **– Pierre Brouard**

When a new team member joins an organisation, there is very often a process of 'reading' them, where their ability to fit into the culture is assessed, and they are quite literally constructed by the organisation as an asset or a liability:

> *So a company will see a young person coming in who is very ambitious, and immediately label them "entitled" instead of saying, "Wow, how can we mentor this awesome individual?"*

> **– Jennie Tsekwa**

---

[11] In the popular formulation of the management studies professor Sumantra Ghoshal.

Corporate culture is experienced by many as frothing with racial mistrust, tensions, hostility and fear. Black workers are often labelled as "incompetent", "tokens", "empty suits" or "Affirmative Action appointments" [12]. Despite the promise of equality, freedom, and dignity codified in the South African Constitution, LGBT workers face considerable homophobia at work [13]. Where different marginalised identities overlap such as in the case of Black women, who are resisted both by white people and Black men reports of discrimination and exclusion are especially acute [14]. Would-be leaders are stereotyped, demonised, encouraged to erase their African identity, and forced into hiding in order to survive in corporate work environments.

When significant portions of the workforce do not feel as if they are valued and experience the corporate culture as a constant assault on their identities, disengagement is the logical result. Low productivity, inefficiency, and other measures of poor performance are strongly associated with these environments:

> *It's easy for people on top to not really know what people experience in their organisations. It's important to create a space where people want to be, where they can be more productive. But if people are feeling uncomfortable in the workplace, if they don't feel valued, then they stop actually wanting to "bring it" to the workplace: their creativity, their innovative ideas. Who wants to do that in a space that abuses you?*

– Haley McEwen

When organisations are "ugly on the inside" it's no exaggeration to refer to abuse. Abuse thrives in the toxicity created by cultures that do not welcome people for who they are, but always seek to mould them into something different [15]. This can manifest as anything from daily 'micro-aggressions' [16] to physical assault and sexual violence.

In daily organisational work, discrimination and favouritism by direct line managers is often cited as a problem by team members, as is a lack of recognition, where good performance is not recognised, or a good idea is used by the boss, but never credited back to staff. Remuneration may be uneven across the same management level, cleaving to raced, gendered, or ableist power structures;

---

[12] See Vuyo Jack's guide to BEE in South Africa (2013) for a discussion of how these stereotypes work. For a discussion of how Black leaders are stereotyped in the United States, see Carton and Rosette (2011).

[13] Detailed case studies in the South African context are offered by Judge and Nel (2008) and Tlou and Schurink (2003).

[14] This phenomenon is described in Cilliers and Stone's (2005) study of the IT sector in South Africa.

[15] To recap the bell hooks quote in the Introduction: the definition of domination is to "possess remake recast" people into a one-size fits all image of human value.

[16] Micro-aggressions include indicators of Otherness and subjugation, such as complimenting people for exhibiting qualities "their group" supposedly lacks (e.g., making good decisions, speaking English well, being hardworking).

promotions will also tend to go to the people who appear closest to the ideal human being: the 'rational', heterosexual, white, cisgendered man and his cohorts who had power historically. These patterns are very often not visible to executives, who will spend considerable energy denying their existence.

> *It is sometimes hard to put your finger on what those practices are that make a person feel excluded. But when you are in the category of the Other, you feel it at a visceral level.*

– Pierre Brouard

The assertion that the existing corporate culture is the only guarantor of success, competitiveness, or continued excellence, forces new entrants into a business into deeply problematic systems that are crafted from a singular paradigm. Spaces to have conversations with other paradigms and other forms of thinking are closed down. Organisational life makes no room for people to share their different stories and histories, meaning that the development of empathy across historical divides is prevented. The momentum for new entrants is in the direction of assimilation to the dominant culture, and not for the culture itself to be defined by the members of the organisation. This culture becomes a system that makes certain bodies feel in place, and others feel out of place. A critical mass of people who have acquiesced to the dominant norm prevents any challenge of the system, and the dominant group has no incentive not to treat newcomers as walkovers.

More often than not, as has been pointed out, the assimilation is unsuccessful and people find themselves at odds with the dominant culture, dissatisfied with their work, and finding ways to share grievances with others. Between the members of teams, trust is eroded; levels of transparency around why things happen go down; people have less incentive to share information. People become suspicious of each other. Relational dysfunction at the individual level coalesces into cliques that attempt to control who has access to certain bits of information and certain privileges. These pockets of resistance may be ways to 'kick up' or 'across' against other powerful cliques. The emergence of these cliques is an indicator of deep malaise.

While the cultural and systemic dimensions of the organisation are felt viscerally by its members, executives very often only start paying attention once a crisis has erupted. Many organisations are like tinderboxes, just waiting to be ignited.

In some cases it might be someone has gotten a promotion: two staff members arrived at the same time, one who's a white person and has had more opportunities than the other; when the Black staff member complains that this was unfair, other staff start saying that actually this is an established pattern within the organisations. The event gives form to the systemic critique, which ultimately reverberates throughout the organisation, and the result is a full-blown crisis.

– Busi Dlamini

2.3.4. The Road-Runner: "Itchy Feet"

Staff disengagement, the early warning sign that an organisation is ugly on the inside, is closely linked to the road-runner phenomenon: team members with "itchy feet" who can't wait to move on to their next job. These "road-runners" are the logical consequence of a negative feedback loop, where bodies that don't fit the dominant culture become the scapegoats for the problem in the first place. The experience of never feeling fully at home, instead of being problematised as a challenge for the organisation to solve, is attributed to the team member: they are framed as being flighty, grasping, or disloyal.

When companies have retention problems, it's a key signal that something's not right:

A further clue that should raise even further alarms is when you can see patterns in the people who are leaving. A lot of companies I work with are not even willing to acknowledge that they actually do not have a problem retaining white males!

– Jennie Tsekwa

Organisations that are in constant competition with each other for skilled employees need to start looking to their own internal problems, rather than laying the blame solely on the shoulders of the highly "marketable" individuals that they struggle to retain. As we explored above, a fixation on keeping up appearances involves treating people not as ends in themselves, but as a means to an end, and in a dehumanising reduction of human complexity to a box-ticking exercise. The extent to which valuable team members are able to feel as if they are part of defining an inclusive internal culture can determine whether or not they decide to stick around. Companies should reflect on their complicity in maintaining historical hierarchies:

If you exclude a group of people from opportunities, then to me it makes perfect sense that when opportunities arrive staff will go for them. To me it does not demonstrate a person's lack of loyalty to the company, or lack of reliability. If there's a country context where for so long corporations have not shown any loyalty to people, or any fairness to people, why must companies turn around and blame people for not being loyal to them?

– Jennie Tsekwa

Blaming employees for structural problems is one of the themes that we will examine in more detail in the remainder of this book. The human resources literature on Black managers suggests a far more nuanced take on the reasons for their decisions to move on[17.] The shorter tenures of many Black managers in corporate leadership roles can often be attributed to organisational hostility towards Black people, and these managers' contrasting desire to feel that they really *do* belong somewhere, where they can add real value, and leave a legacy, rather than being treated as convenient for Employment Equity statistics[18]. Organisations that fail to introspect about the reasons people leave are doomed to repeat the pattern of hiring on valuable staff members who are soon itching to leave.

2.3.5.   The Mastodon: "Too Important to Listen"

The mastodontic organisation is a problem not just for critical diversity practitioners but for any modern management approach that tries to create agile, innovative entities. The mastodontic organisation is hierarchical, almost militaristic; it implements decisions through a top-down chain of command, and its leaders insulate themselves from the demands of their staff. Like the woolly mammoth, this organisation is a relic frozen in a faraway glacier. It is unresponsive, inflexible, and insensitive to the demands of its own members.

While most executives scoff at mastodontic excess, the signs of fossilization are common and shared across many organisations that think of themselves as creative, modern, and responsive. Again, the existence of a mainstream and monolithic corporate culture is at the heart of the problem. Team members are encouraged to leave their own knowledge about how the world works at home, and to sign up to the company way of thinking. This distinction between the knowledges that may be spoken and those that must be kept quiet creates cultures of secrecy and silence. A prime example of this is the way that cultures of male entitlement and sexual violence continue to thrive around the world.

---

[17] Khoele and Daya (2014) identify a range of personal motivations that employers must take into account when hiring and retaining Black managers in knowledge industries. The notion of "job hopping" among Black senior managers has also been critically examined by Nzukuma and Bussin (2011) as well as by Mtungwa (2009).
[18] For deeper analysis of how this organisational hostility plays out, see Kelly, Wale, Soudien, and Steyn (2007).

Knowledge of sexual harassment becomes subjugated knowledge: we know, everybody knows; here are the guys, and we know what they have done. The dynamic of "everybody knows" only becomes repressed knowledge when people don't have access to resources, can't get good lawyers, are not guaranteed another job.

– **Melanie Judge**

The ability to think critically, and the ability to criticise the behaviour of people who hold power, are intimately interwoven. They must be jealously guarded. An organisation becomes mastodontic when it insulates itself to critical voices, either through active silencing, or through failing to provide the resources that are required to allow marginalised voices to be heard. Managers focus on "decreasing the noise" from staff and become comfortable, and complacent, about the status quo.

Members of an organisation that develop ways to listen to each other's concerns, demands, and ideas in mutually respectful and institutionally protected ways not only expose violence and malfeasance within their midst, they also orient the organisation around plural knowledges that may be spoken, and more creative and multifaceted ways of solving problems and reaching organisational objectives. Very often the failure of the mastodontic organisation to solve a problem is down quite simply to the failure of its dominant and dominating system of thought to solve the problem. The solutions, and the knowledges, were in fact there all along.

The opportunity to reflect deeply on the system, and to ask critical questions, positions team members as more than just passive and interchangeable bodies that should be grateful to be in the room. This is, however, anathema to the mastodontic organisation, which demands loyalty, obedience, and gratitude: it splits the consciousness of team members that think differently, forcing them to assume one way of being professional, goal-oriented, committed to doing a good job while at another level being cognisant of the violence being done to other aspects of their being.

For those in powerful positions, who have the most to gain from mastodontic systems, the knowledge that comes from the top down is simply and plainly synonymous with truth; it sets the standard for what the organisation regards as "excellence". There is a fear of cracking the ice around the mammoth: you either commit to excellence (which has worked for you in the past) by accepting the weight of tradition, or you allow people to start chipping away with their criticisms and their alternative ways of thinking through problems. The fear is that the organisation risks everything by questioning its own truth. Throughout organisations we encounter these styles of binary thinking: either excellence or transformation; either high university fees or poor quality education; either appropriately qualified or an affirmative action appointment. Within market logics, the fear quite simply is that any change not explicitly oriented around profitability is a step towards the grave.

The result is that many of these organisations are quite simply 'stuck' in a dated paradigm: unable to change from what they have always been. This 'stuckness' is however not going to last long:

> *When we start to work with organisations, we will most often encounter a usually younger cohort of Black individuals who are trying, often unsuccessfully, to challenge the status quo. Changes have been happening, but these changes have been so incredibly slow with shifts of less than a percentage point year on year that their internal climates are characterised by a strong sense of impatience created by a younger generation. The private sector has yet to experience anything like the kind of revolutionary demands of Fees Must Fall, but that way of thinking definitely will definitely have an impact.*

> **– Busi Dlamini**

2.4.   Conclusion

In this chapter, we have painted a fairly negative picture of the organisation in crisis. The internal impatience of team members, the hunger for tangible change, we've referred to threatens the calm that many executives seek to enforce on their teams. This moment of crisis, characterised by huge scandals and ructions in a wide variety of organisations across sectors and around the world, speaks to a systemic conjuncture: an opportunity to rearticulate our identities and make sense of ourselves as members of society. The 'transformation' project as we have argued has failed to deliver meaningful transformation at all. Organisations manifest the signs of crisis they hide their heads in the sand, try to keep up appearances, maintain ugly internal cultures, haemorrhage skilled staff, and find comfort in mastodontic solidity but often don't act until they are already in a full-scale emergency. In the next chapter, we will look at the history of the organisation, in an attempt to try and diagnose the problem more accurately.

Chapter 3

Poisoned Roots: A Short History of the Organisation

In this chapter, we explore the historical roots of the organisation. *Historicization* is an important step in social analysis because it undermines the taken-for-granted nature of the present, dispelling the illusion of a world that simply has to be the way it is. In understanding the choices that were made, the accidents that happened, and the global shifts that impacted on the development of organisations, we can better understand how the present is open to reinterpretation and to change.

We start in section 1 with a discussion of the broad global currents that impacted on the development of the organisation, reviewing the transition from relatively closed to open and globalised social systems that accompanied European colonialism and the development of modern capitalism. In section 2 we look at how this history played out in South Africa specifically. We then summarise the chapter in the final section.

3.1.   Global 'Modernity'

The crux of historicizing the present is understanding the notion of 'modernity'. What we think of as 'modern' life might seem so obvious as to not really require much thought: people aspire to work for corporations, to consume particular goods, to achieve certain lifestyle aims. These aspects of our lives seem entirely normal and unremarkable. What they however mask in all their common-sense obviousness is specific power relations and the historical developments that have secured for some people a particular set of benefits, and for other people a different set. These differences have subtly infused what we have come to think of as possible. The Argentinian political philosopher Ernesto Laclau argued that the way that we understand our own identities and the world we live in and think of as normal can be thought of as a discursive space that is *intelligible* to us, which has a *horizon*[19]. It is only by going beyond this "horizon of intelligibility" that we can start to imagine worlds different from the one we currently live in, and to open up the possibility of social and political change. What we therefore need in our study of history is a bold

---

[19] Laclau developed the concept of the "horizon of intelligibility" in a number of his writings. See his *New Reflections on the Revolutions of our Time* (1990) for the classic statement. This idea was also significantly developed by the South African theorist (and one-time student of Laclau) Aletta Norval in *Deconstructing Apartheid Discourse* (1996).

kind of imagination—bold because it can see how things might have turned out differently. This is what a lot of sci-fi writing is about: imagining different worlds, possible worlds, in the past or present or future, and populating them with social relations and identities that would make sense within those frameworks. Making social change happen requires that kind of imagination.

3.1.1. Pre-Modern, Modern, Post-Modern

The pre-modern era was characterised by slower migration of knowledge and ideas. People tended to live most of their lives in fairly homogenous groups in terms of language, religion, and ethnicity, and were therefore less likely to be challenged by other worldviews.

In this kind of world, you had a sense of yourself and those of your community as persons. How you understood others, tended to rely on the fantasies of the unconscious. People in western Europe imagined Others beyond the frontiers of their influence as half people, half animals centaurs, or satyrs, or Pan. Faraway lands were imagined to be populated by monstrous people with heads growing out under their arms. Given the relative isolation of human communities, there were few reality checks on such notions. Views like these were not really dangerous to others, as they had little or no impact, except at those quite rare times when groups did come into conflict. These times were of course far from safe, and characterised by war, disease, and short lives for many people around the world.

The modern era is to a large extent synonymous with the colonial era. This is the time of European global expansion, when the waves of globalisation as they were unleashed in the 15th century, initiating the interconnected world we know today. In this world, one cannot in reality understand one part of the globe without understanding how it is linked into the system. During this period, Western European nations gained seafaring and military advantage over other parts of the world. It is important to note that this advantage was historically *contingent* (i.e., based on actions and events that did not have to happen as they did and that could have had different results) and not *inevitable* (i.e., scientifically predictable and necessary). The Europeans were able to insert themselves into the worlds they were encountering in positions of conquest and supremacy. This was basically the era of domination, where the European centres had the power to define others and have their definitions stick. The construction of the Other was still influenced by the notion of the proper human, the superior version of humanity, which was of course European, and everybody else was aberrant, deficient, inferior.

In the era of modernity we see events in parochial Europe send shockwaves through the globe: the Protestant break with the Roman Catholic Church, the rise of capitalism, the Industrial Revolution, and the development of the modern national state. Most particularly, the knowledge systems emerging from the specific group that gained the most power at this time—bourgeois, western European men—created particular notions of truth, knowledge, and science, supported by their own religions traditions. This knowledge explicitly worked to their advantage economically, culturally, ideologically, and politically. Collectively referred to as Eurocentrism, it centred white, Christian, able-bodied, heterosexual men, and suppressed other understandings of the world, creating an ideology of a world order in which the European man was the epitome of intellect, development and achievement, and therefore the rightful overlord of the world system. Even as successive waves of 'Enlightenment' and ensuing world-views in that tradition introduced notions such as the universal rights of 'man' and eventually (after decades of support) contributed to the end of the practice of slavery, to votes for women, and so on, these 'liberties' (in what became the dominant 'liberal' world order) still held the white men at its centre as the epitome of rationality and the most deserving of true human freedom[20].

The tight political and ideological system that held colonial modernity in place has cracked and is still in the process of fragmenting. Other ways of thinking that are antagonistic to ideologies that legitimise the global colonial system of economic power have been developed from other centres of power, including decolonial, anti-capitalist, and other forms of counter-hegemonic critique. These critiques, which pre-date but also inform our era, are now ushering in the postmodern, postcolonial, or decolonial (depending on what view one has of this process).

Wars and struggles for physical decolonization of territories have been succeeded by more fundamental challenges to power relations. The return of the land to Indigenous people in places like the United States and Australia still seems unlikely, however, and the futures of land justice movements around the world hang in the balance. There are now different alignments of powers and spaces, which have been set in motion by other sets of interests to those that have been virtually untouchable until recently, raising the political assertions of those previously conquered. Politically this process can be traced from the Bandung conference of 1955 which initiated the alliance of non-aligned nations, through to new configurations such as BRICS (made of Brazil, Russia, India, China, and South Africa). The extent to which other centres of power represent the possibility for a fundamental break with the past, or are simply old colonial wine in new bottles, remains to be seen.

The process is also visible in the loss of confidence in the claims to universality that have bolstered Western knowledge. The truth claims that legitimised the belief in the unquestioned superiority of the (white, male) West, and the epistemological mechanisms that produced them, are increasingly being challenged and exposed as parochial and self-serving. The axiomatic binary of "the West, and the rest" that dominated this period is being troubled[21]. Of course, there have been subversive knowledges: counter-ideologies always exist. But the world order, understood as

---

[20] For excellent critiques of liberalism, see David Theo Goldberg's *The Racial State* (2001) and the work of philosopher Charles W. Mills, especially *Racial Liberalism* (2008).
[21] This global shift as it pertains to knowledge production is outlined in the book *Theory from the South: Or, how Euro-America is evolving toward Africa* by Jean Comaroff and John L. Comaroff (2012).

having a single centre of authority; one model for understanding the nature of the human, the relationship to the environment, to knowledge as such, to culture, geography, development, to the management of wealth, and more, is increasingly being profoundly challenged. Decolonial thinking is an assertion of the value of the knowledge systems and ways of being originating from the indigenous peoples of the world, with the intention of ushering in a more plural, multi-centred world system. It is fundamentally also a reclamation of dignity.

3.1.2.   Dynamics of the Modern Social Order

We inherited from modernity notions of the appropriate, standard, right, proper, good, and ideal ways of doing and being in relation to each other that were shaped within relations of unequal power. Social relations were imagined, instituted, and bedded down in a social fabric characterised by the domination of everybody else by the positionality that gained the upper hand. As the decolonial scholar Ramon Grosfoguel has pointed out, it was not just capitalism that arrived with the ships of colonisers, but "European/ capitalist/ military/christian/ patriarchal/ white/ heterosexual" males that arrived, establishing "simultaneously (spatially and temporally) several entangled global hierarchies"[22]. Below, we will discuss some key aspects of this interlinked web of power relations under their rubrics as *West/Eurocentric, White supremacist, Colonialist, Heteropatriarchal, Christo-normative, Capital(abl)ist, Nationalist,* and *Anthropocentric.*

- *West/Eurocentrism*

As Western Eurocentrism became powerful all over the globe, it constructed its understanding of the world through a binary lens with the European self at the centred position, and all others at the margins. Not all European people were equally powerful in the modern-colonial era, of course. Western Europeans had enslaved each other and people from Eastern Europe prior to the enslavement of African people. People from the eastern and southern regions of Europe were regarded with some disdain, as lesser Europeans. Class hierarchies persist to the present day. The point here however is that knowledge itself was understood as European, and it reflected, normalised and naturalised the self-image of (an elite group of) Western Europeans as the most advanced, civilised, and generally superior people of the world.

---

[22] This quote is from Grosfoguel's important article "A Decolonial Approach to Political-Economy: Transmodernity, Border Thinking and Global Coloniality" (2009, p. 18).

- ### *White Supremacy*

One of the most important cogs in the machinery that created modernity was the construction of the notion of 'race' as a way to mark the separateness of the Europeans from the other people of the world. Whiteness and Blackness were not categorizations given by nature, but political categories that enabled the division of the world into superior and inferior peoples, naturalizing notions of the more and less deserving and enabling inequality to be institutionalized within the nation state[23]. The racial bias in the global system of modernity should not be mistaken for a layer of injustice overlaid upon a basically just system. It was constitutive of the system, at the level of the very DNA of modernity[24].

- ### *Colonialism*

Between 1492 and 1914, European countries conquered and dominated 84 percent of the surface area of the globe[25]. This expansion was accompanied by the migration of millions of Europeans to other parts of the world, and accompanied by the forceful imposition of the European will: genocides, land dispossession, the imposition of various kinds of unfree labour and slavery, systematic exploitation of the natural resources for the benefit of the metropolitan areas, the decimation of indigenous languages, beliefs and cultures, and undermining of local ways of knowing. Political systems were introduced to govern indigenous people as subjects, not as citizens[26].

- ### *Heteropatriarchalism*

Part of the system of privileging men in Europe was the development of a particular gender order. It entailed the subordination of women within the home, each woman serving a man, caring for him and his children within this nuclear family arrangement. She did the unpaid labour, providing service and support and remaining economically dependent, which allowed him to be economically active and to engage in the public and political domain, and to achieve recognition and rewards and remain in control of his family.

These gender roles were aligned with sex differences, which were understood to be a simple binary male and female and acceptable sexuality was understood to be exclusively heterosexual. Any other kind of sexual expression was disapproved of,

---

[23] For a compelling treatment of this process, see Achille Mbembe's *Critique of Black Reason* (2017), especially Chapter 1 (pp 10-36).
[24] For a book-length explanation of why this is the case, the classic reference is *The Racial Contract* (1997) by the American philosopher Charles W. Mills.
[25] Philip T. Hoffman. *Why Did Europe Conquer the World?* (2015).
[26] This is the central argument advanced by Ugandan political theorist Mahmood Mamdani in his *Citizen and Subject: Decentralized Despotism and the Legacy of Late Colonialism* (1997).

and usually outlawed. The variations, continuities and continuums of sexuality and gender were not acknowledged.

The different ways of expressing gender, sexuality or family that the Europeans encountered elsewhere were seen as evidence of racial backwardness[27]. Part of the colonial project was to teach the indigenous people to do gender, sexuality, marriage, and family in the "respectable" European way.

- *Christo-Normativism*

Integral to Eurocentrism was the sense that all others needed to be remade to conform with European establishment, even if they would never quite achieve the same fit as the genuine European. As the religion of western Europe, Christianity was also exported as part of the "civilizing" mission. It was seen as the only true religion, the belief systems of other people were cast as superstitions or heretical and a threat to civilized values. The power of Christo-normativity led to the conversion of millions of people across the globe to Christianity, and also to resistance from other religions that were cast as of lesser value or backward.

- *Capit(abl)ism*

Capitalism drove colonial conquest, with an ever-expanding need for new markets, more and cheaper labour, and resources. Capitalism prioritises profit, wealth accumulation and private ownership. And it brought about a particular class system, which includes the owner class and the labouring/working classes, and increasingly creates surplus people for whom there is no place in the economic system.

The category of "disabled" is a product of the capitalist system. The term came into existence with the industrial revolution, when all those who couldn't do a day's work in the factory were categorized together as "disabled". Before that people would have been seen as blind, or deaf, or "crippled" but they would have been accommodated in more, or less, satisfactory ways within the community. Once capitalism became the "normal" system, people with impairments would all belong to the group of those seen as unable to be self-sufficient, independent; as (burdensome) surplus people who were more or less destined to be economically marginalized.

- *Nationalism*

Modernity developed in tandem with the nation state. Originally the nation state was conceptualized as a 'homeland,' under a single government, for a group of people,

---

[27] See Sally Kitch's (2009) study of the imbrication of the racial and heteropatriarchal orders in the United States, and Anne McClintock's (1995) book *Imperial Leather* which shows how the construction of sexuality and gender within the family context was a key dimension of the project of British colonialism and imperialism. See also Acker (2004).

and understood as a bounded territory for a population homogenous in terms of language, religion and ethnicity. Those not part of the dominant group, were subordinated, invisiblised and often assimilated into the dominant ways of being, failing which, they faced various forms of neglect and marginalisation.

Within the nation state, the political philosophy that gained predominance was various expressions of human liberalism, which emphasizes the relationship of the individual to the state, and the separation of church from state. Implicitly, all nations have been judged by how they match up to the ideals of liberalism. The downside of this philosophy is that it does not recognize the "groupiness" of society, how structurally groups of people are unequally positioned in relation to each other; it hides dominance and social privilege and interprets life trajectories in terms of individual effort and worth.

Increasingly, the nation state is losing its position in world affairs; many multinational companies often have more money, influence and power than many states; transnationality is becoming more and more the way in which matters are decided.

3.1.3. Capitalism, Competition, and the 'Survival of the Fittest'

From the mid-nineteenth century, thinking about human social life became highly influenced by Charles Darwin's theory of biological evolution by natural selection. Whereas Darwin's theory offered an explanation for how plant and animal species had evolved historically, so-called "Social Darwinists" projected natural selection into the future as a model for the gradual improvement of human society, where the fact that only the 'fittest' would survive served as an important moral indication of their superiority. It was the discursive shift around 'survival' which moved from a biological description to a normative prescription and the perversion of the concept of evolutionary 'fitness' into a system of social hierarchization, that laid the groundwork for some of the worst atrocities of the modern age.

Colonialism and capitalism acquired a 'scientific' grounding through the notion that it was only through competition that humanity would improve. A moral obligation to weed out the weaker elements of the population whether 'backward' and 'savage' people in distant lands, or 'degenerate' or 'disabled' people in the colonial metropoles was thereby elaborated. We can observe that various logics of oppression grew from this moral obligation: the logic of 'inferior' races; the logic of white women's reproductive responsibility and of the degeneracy of non-heterosexual sex; the logic of seeing only fully 'able' bodies as valuable and desirable in the future; and various cultural chauvinisms that centre (northern) European and American ways of thinking, talking, and being.

The construction of race specifically built on earlier Linnaean models of different 'sub-species' (with a taxonomy that infamously divided 'Caucasians' from Africans and 'Mongoloids') combined with both biological and social Darwinism to create a 'scientific' edifice of the study of 'race biology'. It was the biological/natural reality of difference between races that was supposedly responsible for the different levels of 'development' found in different parts of the globe. Since the 1950s, actual study of the human genome based on understanding the role of DNA has led geneticists to conclude that there is no such thing as separate 'races' from a genetic point of view. Genetic differences between people who are seen as African are often larger than between people who come from supposedly the 'same' race group[28]. What seem like large differences in appearance do not map onto the kinds of genetic regularities that race biologists asserted they did. And yet race biology has yet to be abandoned as a research project, largely because of the huge possessive investment of so many researchers who believe there must be 'something' there. A similar afterlife is observable in the project of eugenics. Historically, 'inferior' people were coerced or forced into sterilization or abortion by white supremacists. Race 'hygiene' one of the euphemistic synonyms used for eugenic atrocities was implemented on a continuum that ranged from genocide (in Namibia, Australia, the US, and the Holocaust of the Jews of Europe) to related forms of annihilation, often of Indigenous peoples, including separating children from their parents, forced adoption, education that asserted the supremacy of a particular language or canon, and dismissing as barbarism anything not considered having attained an 'advanced' enough level of cultural sophistication.

What we think of as the 'corporation' under capitalism was forged when these ideas were still very much *en vogue*. The father of the modern factory, Henry Ford, was a committed eugenicist and 'scientific' racist. While his more extreme ideas are perhaps out of fashion, the patterns of thinking that govern life within many corporations a 'sink or swim' mentality, summary dismissals, attempts to maximise profit through minimising labour costs, necessitating blank hostility to labour organising are all founded on the idea that the corporation is like a body competing for survival with other bodies and that its only imperative is to survive. The Latin root of 'corporation' is after all the word for body, *corpus*.

Of course, nobody would expect an organisation to be interested in its own demise. The problem with this ideology is not that survival should not be a priority, but that the maximisation of the self-interest of the business trumps all other concerns.

This way of thinking about organisations obscures both the bodies within the body the people in the company, who are ends in themselves and have lives and aspirations that must be taken into account and the bodies outside of the body other stakeholders, society at large, the profound interconnectedness of human social life, as well as the abundance of non-human life.

What the modern age has left over from Social Darwinism is the idea that it is our responsibility to defeat and to conquer the weak and that profit profit at any cost is in fact the moral responsibility of a company. The ideology that states that a company's

---

[28] An excellent exposé of the inaccuracies and dishonesties of race biology and eugenics in the past and the present is Angela Saini's, *Inferior: the return of race science* (2019).

only responsibility is to maximise value for its shareholders is still pervasive and powerful. Because of the economic history of the world and the development of trade, often along the lines set down by colonial domination, this profit still tends to accrue to the West; and generally within countries to the white, male, 'rational' thinker who carries 'pure' genes. He is seen as the most competitive, the most powerful, the very embodiment of intelligence. Those whose labour must be valued as low as possible in order for the company to survive tend to not be of this group: they are women who take time off to have babies, 'unskilled' Black people, or people who are 'disabled' by the logic of capitalism.

The idea that human value in a corporate setting is reducible to their contribution to the bottom line is of course far from transparent. Because societies have centred the value of white men for so long, white men may appear valuable, even when without any substance. Medical patients, for example, who prefer to be treated by a white man, when a Black woman specialist could have saved their lives, are the victims of a social illusion: the illusion of white competence, intelligence, and trustworthiness. Companies may likewise undermine their own competitiveness by falling for this illusion. Very often, the 'value' of a person in a corporate setting turns out to be entirely socially produced: they are trusted because they are male and not because they are trustworthy; they listen to them because they are white and not because they have anything of value to say.

One would expect management theory to have adopted a more critical view of the social production of the corporation, and of notions such as 'competence' but, with the exception of small but growing fields such as critical management studies, this has not been the case. In most business schools, the colonial formulae are merely reproduced. Students are not trained in broader social theories and systems, but instead trained to replicate and reproduce an inherently racist model.

Management ideology is not just reproduced in boardrooms and business schools; it structures international relations. 'Developing' nations are pressured by the West to have particular kinds of policies that secure advantageous access to trade opportunities for dominant powers. So-called 'overseas development assistance' (ODA) very often consists in creating new opportunities for metropolitan for- and non-profit companies to extend into or maintain their influence in distant societies. The notion of evolution through competition forces the 'Global South' into zero-sum relations with each other, with the result that colonised economies continue not to be able to sustain themselves, remaining in the position of existing to sustain other, more established, economies.

3.2.   The Development of the Organisation in South Africa

Let us now turn to a specific country example, and one that is close to our hearts: South Africa. The way these global processes played out in this colonial context are, we would argue, especially relevant not only to understanding why the project of 'transformation' post-1994 has stalled in the country today, but also to understanding other contexts that are haunted by the memory of European colonisation, and have persistent racial orders. It is worth remembering, as a starting point, that it was not really a foreign government that sent Jan van Riebeeck to establish a 'refreshment' station at the Cape of Good Hope in 1652: it was a multinational corporation, the Dutch East India Company (*Vereenigde Oostindische Compagnie*, or VOC). The VOC had quasi-governmental powers with enormous political, economic, and military authority, which included rights to establish trade relations with native peoples throughout the lands surrounding the Indian Ocean and East Asia, initiate tax rules, extract labour, forge wars, sign treaties, design and implement laws, and dispense justice[29]. Van Riebeeck was the first in a long line of profiteers.

On his arrival at the Cape, van Riebeeck initiated trade relations with the native Khoi people, but when these failed to deliver the kinds of results he had envisioned, he obtained permission from the VOC directors to enslave them. He stated at the time that he considered them "idle, godless savages" and a "brutal gang living without any conscience"[30] This (re)construction of human difference in relation to European modes of being, where Europeans were constructed as normal humans and Indigenous people as something else, was typical of most colonial encounters. The discursive construction of what a 'proper human' (and also, at the time, good Christian) was served as the fuel that justified colonial conquest, enslavement and exploitation of native people as free labour in service of white European corporate capital.

From an Indigenous perspective, what really changed after slavery was outlawed in the 19th century? The new labour relations arguably merely used a different set of laws and punishments to achieve a similar end: white settler domination. White intra-settler politics hinged on who would be able to control the labour and the wealth of the land. The emergent 'Afrikaner' identity of early Dutch settlers clashed with the new scions of British liberalism over whether native peoples were to be regarded as customers for Western goods (and should therefore be allowed to join the world of money as 'free' labourers) or were to be kept in a perpetual state of slavery to their masters[31]. The "Great Trek" into the interior was largely a reaction to what was seen as the encroachment of liberalism. In their newly established republics, the "Boers" set about legislating a strict racial order: according to the Zuid-Afrikaansche Republiek's Constitution of 1858, for example, it was made clear that "there shall be no equality between whites and blacks in church or state"[32].

---

[29] For a global review of the economics of colonialism, see Andy Baker's (2014) book "Shaping the Developing World: The West, the South, and the Natural World".

[30] See Nicole Ulrich's (2016) account of the history of this time.

[31] The classic historical account of the roots of the racial order in South Africa is offered in Timothy J. Keegan's *Colonial South Africa and the Origins of the Racial Order* (1997). The British liberal position did of course also have a moral argument against slavery, but the driving logic, argues Keegan, was one of inclusion in markets.

[32] See Anthony W. *Marx's Making Race and Nation* (1998) for an account of this process.

It is in this racist context that settlers asserted their rights over the diamond fields in what came to be called "Kimberly" and, later, the goldfields of the "Witwatersrand", ushering in the era of massive new corporations such as Anglo-American and De Beers with their financiers in the markets of Western Europe. The annexation of the Boer republics by the British, although given a paternalistic sheen by apologists who claimed the British were protecting the amaZulu and other ethnic groups from Boer tyranny, was essentially a land-grab of some of the world's most valuable territory. Since then, South Africa's political narrative has to a large extent revolved around what is right for "the economy," and labour markets have been structured to maximise the extraction of resources, the entrenchment of a monopoly of white capital, and its underpinnings in a racist, sexist, ableist, heteronormative, and otherwise hierarchical social system.

3.2.1. The Colonial Division of Labour

The rich mineral bearing diamond and gold deposits were in deep level hard-rock, which meant that mines had a high demand for manual labour. Corporations thus worked together with state power to ensure that a steady stream of Black men from rural areas was available to work as migrant labourers, for as little as possible, ensuring maximum productivity and profits[33]. Men would only leave their homesteads if they were forced to, and to achieve this end a system of coercion that included the so-called "hut tax" was implemented within the colonial system that ensured that men streamed into the mining centres, without their wives and children[34]. The creation of same-sex hostels in the urban centres entrenched the notion of the rural areas as a "reservoir" of labour that men were supposed to return to once a year to see to their roles as patriarchs. The forced migrancy of Black labour has been identified as lying at the centre of a plethora of the social ills of modern-day South Africa. This process of dispossession, dislocation, and the conversion of human subjects into human resources, tore apart homes, families, and entire societies in the name of profit. It created a gendered division of labour in which women were relegated to the domestic sphere, a practice that was sanctified by the Christian missionary schooling system. The racist, heteropatriarchal, Christonormative, capital(abl)ist dimensions of the global order thus achieved a specific intensity in South Africa.

Alienation from the land ensured both by war, trickery, and successive pieces of racist legislation that made it impossible for tenants to survive as farmers ensured that Black people were easily relegated to a class of manual labourers on mines and white farms. Many Afrikaners and other working class whites who had moved to the mines

---

[33] See Visser (2007) for an account of how the racialized division of labour has permanently affected the union movement in South Africa, and the way that class struggle is envisioned and actualized.
[34] For a comprehensive history of the movement of labour into the cities and the formation of the racialized economy of South Africa see Nigel Worden's *The Making of Modern South Africa* (2012).

from around the world also found themselves without land, and without protection against the behemoth corporations that emerged in South Africa. Early white working class political action thus set about establishing a labour movement for white people that would set them apart from Black labour. The Communist party slogan of the early twentieth century was "Workers of the World Unite for a White South Africa!"[35]. The first colour bars for jobs were implemented in the late 19th and early 20th centuries, excluding black African workers from certain job roles. Corporations, with the prodding of government, set about creating unequal human resource regimes, where notions of white superiority and black inferiority were introduced as characteristic of South African labour. This was largely because whites feared that Black people who were more numerous—posed too much competition to them. Whites thus positioned themselves as a "labour aristocracy"[36] and correspondingly, all black workers cast into a pool of unskilled, cheap labour.

3.2.2.   The Apartheid Order

While the world's attention was focused on Paris in 1948, and the adoption of the Universal Declaration of Human Rights, the National Party had just come to power in South Africa and was setting about recycling European racial pseudoscience into a complex, modern, and multifaceted system of division: apartheid. Apartheid divided the country into racialised hierarchies that legislated white superiority and black subjugation. The apartheid regime asserted that God had imbued whiteness with sophisticated intellectual capabilities, power, responsibility and authority to rule over its Black subjects. Apartheid was institutionalised through the promulgation and enforcement of more than a hundred violent segregationist laws that were passed between 1948 and 1980 covering the spheres of economy, spatial organisation, education, healthcare, labour, and social relations; to a large extent, these laws continue to shape social life in South Africa[37].

These laws unjustly centred white, heterosexual, able-bodied masculinity as the ideal human form, legitimating the dominance of this positionality in relation to society, the economy, and the resources of the land. So-called "non-white" people were placed in a perpetual position of dependence on their white masters. Access to "white" areas, which accounted for over 80% of South Africa, and movement within them, was severely restricted, including through the Urban Areas Consolidation Act of 1945, which required Blacks to always carry their "pass" documents around with them, which came to be popularly referred to as the "dompas". Homosexuality was

---

[35] Jeremy Krikler has written about how early socialist movements in South Africa promoted white supremacy in *The Rand Revolt: the 1922 insurrection and racial killing in South Africa* (2005).

[36] This is Visser's (2007) term.

[37] The authors of *Race Trouble: Race, Identity and Inequality in Post-Apartheid South Africa* (Durrheim et al., 2011) show how these pieces of legislation continue to shape the post-apartheid order.

classified as a crime, and the system also worked to exclude women from positions of power[38] and economic independence.

Conscious of the centrality of access to quality education for meaningful economic participation, the key apartheid figure, Hendrik Verwoerd, engineered the extension of a particularly virulent form of education to Black people, one that attempted to inculcate into generations of schoolchildren that there was no place for them in the economy above the level of certain forms of physical labour and service. According to Verwoerd, Africans had opportunities in their own communities and it was thus futile to train them for meaningful roles in the European community. He extended this 'Bantu Education' system, which surpassed and supplanted missionary schools, foreclosing the notion of intellectual development in favour of a pipeline of cheap, unskilled labour, thereby sustaining and perpetuating an unequal relation for 'non-European' children to their white peers.

The role played by corporations and Western European governments in financing apartheid cannot be ignored. The emergence of neoliberalism in the 1970s and early 1980s, when Ronald Reagan and Margaret Thatcher were at the helms of government in the USA and the UK, saw the corporation's leading role in public life become hegemonic[39]. South Africa was for the neo-liberals a bulwark against Communism. So, while the political and economic powers of the West at the time were not hostile to white supremacy *per se*[40]; it was the political organisation of their consumers and voters that pressured them from below to implement economic and cultural sanctions against the apartheid government. While these sanctions were instrumental in forcing the apartheid government to the negotiating table in the 1980s and 1990s, the neoliberal consensus, cemented by the collapse of the Soviet Union, meant that any thoroughgoing attempt to redistribute the wealth of South Africa its land and the fruits of its mineral and other wealth to make up for centuries of racialised oppression, was simply not an option. South Africa's transition to multiracial democracy was to be entirely market-led, and to entrenching existing distributions of property.

3.2.3. How "Post" is Post-Apartheid, Really?

After the formal demise of apartheid in 1994, the new democratically-elected government took on the momentous task of dismantling colonial laws and structures, ushering in an era of nation building. A number of transformative strategies emerged:

---

[38] Lize Booysen (2007) points out that in the 50 years of apartheid rule only six white women were ever elected to parliament.

[39] There are a number of critiques of Thatcherism and Reaganism that show how many of the world's present crises have their roots in these ideologies (see e.g. Jones, 2015; Tauss, 2017).

[40] The power, complicity and culpability of large corporations in funding and sustaining oppression in South Africa is captured well by Ron Nixon's book *Selling Apartheid* (2015). Nixon explicates the intricate relationship between Washington, London, Bonn, and Pretoria, and the weighty chequebook exchanges to support white minority power and the oppression of Black majority.

The Reconstruction and Development Program (RDP) in 1994, the Growth, Employment and Redistribution (GEAR) strategy in 1996, the Accelerated and Shared Growth Initiative for South Africa (ASGISA) in 2006, and the National Development Plan (NDP) in 2012. These plans have had uneven success in terms of racial redress and have not significantly affected the lived experiences of the millions of mostly Black people still living in poverty.

The GEAR, ASGISA, and NDP strategies, and to a lesser extent the RDP, are all indicative of a fundamental shift away from Marxist-oriented ideologies within the ruling African National Congress, and towards the neoliberal ideologies established in the time of Thatcher and Reagan. These political strategies can be understood as emerging from the spirit of the times: business leaders sat down at the negotiating table with politicians and had a significant effect on the resulting discourse [41]. Business proactively aligned itself with the ANC and advocated for a language of Black economic empowerment (BEE), which was to take place under more or less free market principles. The BEE programme that emerged focused narrowly on the recruitment of Black individuals, most of whom were connected to the ANC, into executive echelons and onto boards of directors. BEE shares were offered to a politically-connected black elite in the name of supporting black entrepreneurship.

Former Marxists were thus effectively recruited as advocates of free markets, and a radical programme of redistribution was shelved. Even the RDP was seen as too left-wing, and the adoption of GEAR under President Thabo Mbeki created a regulatory environment to attract foreign direct investment, coupled with large-scale privatisation of government-controlled assets to profit oriented corporations. GEAR was envisaged as leading to imminent economic vibrancy, job creation, and social development; it was indeed very effective at bringing foreign money into South Africa, and at establishing South Africa as a gateway for investment in Africa, but it also set the pattern for so-called "jobless growth", where more money in the economy had little impact on employment levels and on social inequality.

Transformative labour laws were intended by the ANC to force corporations to do more to fight inequality. They were also intended to eradicate unfair labour practices and discrimination. These laws include the Broad Based Black Economic Empowerment Act No. 53 (2003), Employment Equity Act No. 55 (1998), Skills Development Act No. 54 (1998), the Labour Relations Act (1998) and the Basic Conditions of Employment Act No. 75 (1997). These policies continue to shape transformation discourses in South Africa's corporate sector.

After 1994, some corporates implemented limited affirmative action programmes, though many of these failed due to their diverse, unstructured, often

---

[41] The impact on the post-apartheid order of business ideologies described here can be explored in more depth in the scholarship of Patrick Bond (1998), Deborah Posel (2010), and Scott Taylor (2007) and Nceba Ndzwayiba (2017), among many others.

shallow and voluntary nature [42]. Voluntary affirmation programmes resulted in corporates giving preferential treatment to white women. The government's structured and prescriptive approach was codified in the Employment Equity Act (1998). The Act recognises that due to apartheid and other related practices and policies, there are disparities in employment, occupation, and income within the national labour market and that these disparities create such pronounced disadvantages for certain categories of people that they cannot be redressed simply by repealing discriminatory laws. The Act states its intentions as promoting equality, eliminating discrimination, promoting diversity, and enabling fair competition on an equal footing. Section 43 of the Act grants powers to the Director General (DG) of the Department of Labour to conduct reviews to determine the extent to which employer organisations comply with the provisions of the Act, and section 30, enables the Commission for Employment Equity (CEE), whose reports on representation in various levels of management we encountered in Chapter 2.

In the 20 years since the Act was promulgated, little has changed in South African corporations. While organisational diversity strategies and practices have yielded some results at the lower levels of occupancy as far as demographic representivity is concerned, corporations have remained largely untransformed at the level of leadership.

The post-apartheid order has also had little effect on income inequality. The burden of inequality has continued to fall squarely on the poor and the marginalised[43]. The rich are able to save enough of their disproportionately high earnings to ensure that their stock of capital always grows at least as fast as the economy; they can also move their money offshore to a variety of tax havens. South Africa has the highest income inequality in the world, even amongst emerging and developing economies. In addition to the skills deficit and high unemployment levels amongst the black majority, real wages have remained stagnant among the poorest labourers, while the income of the highest earners continues to increase.

Given the specific history of capitalism in South Africa it should be unsurprising that the owners of capital in South Africa are primarily white and male. They are also over-represented in the rich lists: men like Christo Wiese, Johann Rupert, and Nicky Oppenheimer, have wealth that equals that of the poorest 50% of the population. Even at the same level of management and in the same jobs, white people still tend to earn more than their Black counterparts [44]. The Employment Equity Act requires organisations to promote diversity through equal treatment of all groups. However, research shows that black workers, women, people with disabilities, and LGBTI workers are not treated equally and fairly in organisations. These groups often

---

[42] See Burger and Jafta's analysis of the history of affirmative action in South Africa (2010).

[43] This phenomenon is analysed in detail by Joel Netshitenzhe (2014).

[44] The South African research company Analytico analysed the salaries of tens of thousands of employees in 2016 and discovered "shocking" pay gaps (Peyper, 2016).

encounter many challenges as they integrate into and intersect with dominant groups in corporate spaces[45].

3.3.   Conclusion

The preceding discussion of both the global and local histories of organisations illustrates that contemporary inequalities in society and in the labour market are entwined with politics. It should be clear that "keeping politics out" of business is a fruitless quest: not addressing politics in the corporate space merely means reproducing the politics of the past, a politics that tried to set a very narrow definition of what it means to be human. Key institutions, companies, schools, universities, and non-profits have historically been central to the production, reproduction, and institutionalisation of oppressive discourses.

---

[45] Many of these experiences are outlined in "Being different together" (Steyn, 2010)

Chapter 4

The Evolution of Approaches to Diversity

The twentieth century, in particular, saw the mushrooming of new fields that tried to make the modern organisation and organisational life the subject of academic investigation. The development of management 'science' the fields of business administration, industrial psychology, and various other disciplines that have taken on the challenge of accounting for the specific dynamics of human social life in its organisational context has been an achievement very much representative of its age. Along with other social and political changes in the twentieth century, management science has also taken on the 'problem' of diversity; in fact, much of the social debate over difference has been framed in terms of the way that it plays out in organisational life.

In this chapter, we review the historical development of these academic approaches to diversity. As diversity practitioners, we are often called into situations where a previous project has adopted one of these frames we are about to lay out and it hasn't quite worked. We offer some reasons why. At the same time, there can be a tendency to scapegoat diversity interventions instead of the underlying social systems that structure difference in the workplace. As such, bad-mouthing different approaches to diversity can reflect a desire to deflect attention from one's own complicity in ongoing structures of discrimination and inequality. So while it may be fair to say that previous models served different ideological aims, or missed the point in terms of the way they were structured, this does not mean that nothing good might have come out of them; only that diversity has remained a tough nut to crack for many organisations around the world.

4.1. Seven Approaches to 'Managing' Diversity

Many organisations and institutions enter into the transformation terrain through a focus on 'diversity'. There are many ways of defining diversity and how it is understood in a given context has a significant impact on the potential for deep transformation. In what follows, we will outline seven different paradigmatic approaches to difference in organisations and sketch out some of the main critiques of these paradigms. Of course, different paradigms can inform specific diversity interventions[46]. What the approaches below have in common is the assumption of "managerial instrumentalism" i.e., that the organisation as a closed system, whose efficient and effective operation trumps other objectives, and that dealing with social justice aims such as inequality is only valuable to the extent that it meets the objectives of the business as previously defined[47].

The managerial instrumentalism paradigm is mainly influenced by North American management theory, which is steeped in the neoliberal ideologies of capital accumulation, developmentalism, globalism, and multiculturalism. Conventional theories of organisational diversity within the management and economics paradigm in South Africa and elsewhere are hugely influenced by this context. This connection is critical for taking into consideration the global power structures and ideologies that produce such theories and the interests furthered. For this reason, much of the history that we will discuss centres on political developments in the United States. What becomes clear in this history is how ideologies of diversity evolved from a social justice orientation during the civil rights era as a veil for capitalist interests. These replaced social justice ideals with profit-centred theories of organisational diversity. These include affirming diversity, diversity management and multiculturalism, the psychosocial theory, the socialisation hypothesis, inclusion, and the theory of "corporate social responsibility".

4.1.1. Affirmative Action and Civil Rights in the United States

The early 1960s were a time of relatively rapid social progress in the United States, and the passage of the Civil Rights Act in 1964, and other progressive laws, emanated from the increasing pressure and demands exerted by movements for equality and social justice following decades of racial discrimination and marginalisation of African Americans and other minority groups, especially Indigenous Americans, in mainstream society and the economy. Prior to this point, the domination of white men in the workplace was more or less taken for granted in many contexts[48]. After 1964, unequal access to voter registration, as well as segregation in workplaces, and other public institutions in the US, was faced with opposition on legal grounds.

In the mid-1960s, President Lyndon B. Johnson was a vocal advocate of equality-oriented policies, proclaiming that it was unfair to simply unbridle a person that had been chained for years, and expect them to compete fairly with others that were never

---

[46] In *Social Change or Status Quo? Approaches to diversity training* (2001), Patti de Rosa argues that implicit assumptions about difference, about what is 'normal', and about openness to changing the status quo are encoded in different approaches to training. As you will see, some of the approaches are unable to analyse the power relations attached to difference, and therefore are ill-equipped to challenge inequality.
[47] "Managerial instrumentalism" has been the foil to many attempts to make workplaces more equal and just environments (see Healy, 2016).
[48] For a comprehensive discussion of this era and the diversity ideologies rooted in it, see Nkomo and Hoobler (2014).

chained. He argued that the most profound form of civil rights lay not in freedom without opportunity or the ability to access such opportunity; not in equality as "a right and a theory but equality as a fact and equality as a result"[49]. In US history, this was one of the few times when positive discrimination, or preferential treatment of minority groups in the human resource processes of recruitment, promotion, development and remuneration, was explicitly politically supported as a strategy to reduce inequalities.

Affirmative action was thus positioned as both a moral and a legal obligation. Similar policies gained ground around the world from the 1960s onwards. Reactions to affirmative action policies have varied substantially among academics, politicians, businesses, and civil society. In South Africa, these contestations tend to follow one of three standpoints: a paradigmatic, a legal, or a pragmatic perspective [50]. Paradigmatic arguments tend to support affirmative action, arguing that its success is dependent on the very object the policy seeks to achieve, which is to shift individual, group and organisational beliefs about diversity and difference. They argue that AA programmes shift the organisational demographics and facilitate the reengineering of organisational practices and systems to value diversity. As a result, their studies tend to focus on examining the pre-conditions for successfully implementing affirmative action policy.

Legal scholars on the other hand approach affirmative action as the site of a 'natural' tension between the values of individual merits, liberties and responsibilities on one hand, and group-focused affirmative programmes on the other. Many traditional liberals argue that race and gender are not adequate grounds for positive discrimination, and that affirmative action confuses the issue by giving all individuals in a group preferential treatment, whether or not they actually have experienced previous discrimination, or have benefited from unjust laws, and so it is actually unfair to hold individuals from "privileged" groups back in favour of those from other groups.

Pragmatists, on the other hand, debate the efficacy of affirmative action in redressing institutionalised racism, the processes and effects of affirmative action strategies in organisations, employee perceptions of and social attitudes towards affirmative action, and the advantages and disadvantages of AA on organisational outcomes and (race) group dynamics, often finding that policies alone are not sufficient to change the internal dynamics of organisations.

Where organisations are faced with the requirements of AA or BEE, they aim to meet legal requirements pertaining to diversity in its context. Where they do this well, this includes the strict monitoring of recruitment, promotion and training opportunities. In this understanding of diversity, 'difference' is essentially treated as a problem that must be solved. The ideology that antagonises this process is the notion

---

[49] This quote is from his commencement speech at Howard University; see Murphy (1995).
[50] See Anne Leonard's (2004) dissertation for a review of the South African context.

of the 'colour-blind' organisation. The supposed ability not to be able to 'see' colour is very often mere cover for attempts to thwart the uncovering of discriminatory processes. Where access to power and resources is differently distributed, and reward and punishment within the organisational setting cleaves to social differences, 'colour-blindness' becomes insensitivity to injustice. In order to be able to deal with inequalities within organisations, they simply have to be measured and managed. If the conditions of their existence are denied, it is impossible to do anything about their results.

The AA paradigm has proven valuable in that it sets clear targets, a clear societal expectation of outcomes, and expects organisations to meet those requirements. It is undoubtedly a *necessary* part of dealing with difference, but also not a *sufficient* one to get organisations to actually change. The South African experience, as we discussed in Chapter 2, provides reason to believe that the existence of legislation and monitoring is not enough to produce the required impact. This does not mean that the law is not important, however.

4.1.2. The Neoliberal Triumph: Affirming Diversity

The end of state-driven social change through regulating business came swiftly when Ronald Reagan came to power in 1980[51]. 'Reaganomics' ushered in a new socio-political hegemony where businesses would be let off their regulatory leashes supposedly to address the "stagflation" (a combination of high unemployment and persistent high inflation) of the 1970s. The result was an intensified conservative white male backlash against AA. White men indeed had the most to gain from the economic and political that emerged under the neoliberalism of Ronald Reagan and Margaret Thatcher [52].

Neoliberal policymaking dramatically weakened organised labour, which had to a limited extent served as an historical counterbalance to capitalist power. AA was increasingly framed as a burden to the state and to business. Retreating from Lyndon Johnson's powerful analysis of the importance of substantive equality and the policy instruments necessary to secure it, Reaganism asserted that race, ethnicity, and sex had come to *replace* ability and qualifications as the way to get into a company or into education, rather than serve as *factors* in assessing structural progress towards equality.

Reagan's focus on 'meritocracy' was tied to race and gender-neutrality (re)conceptualisations of AA that sought to prevent supposed "reverse discrimination"[53]. This neutrality aligned with a particular conception of American fairness, equality, and democracy, i.e., one that celebrated unbridled individual

---

[51] For an account of how affirmative action became "affirming diversity" see Kelly and Dobbin (1998).

[52] For a review of this era, its main ideas, and its influence in the present, see Evans and Sewell, Jr. (2013).

[53] Berry (2007) discusses the intrusion of some of these ideas into the present.

freedom, and ignored the country's history of colonial land theft, slavery, and discrimination. The administrations of George H.W. Bush and Bill Clinton in the 1990s similarly pursued a "affirming diversity" policy as opposed to affirmative action thereby continuing to weaken enforcement and a judicial support for equal opportunity legislation. Bill Clinton specifically advocated for the shift from AA to "managing diversity" to diminish any possible associations with this now unpopular term[54].

It is in this broader context that R. Roosevelt Thomas declared in the Harvard Business Review[55] in 1990 that AA was based on an old set of premises in need of revision in multicultural societies. He argued that AA was parochial and simplifying, and that it in fact worked to amplify gender and racial differences, justifying its abandonment. He argued that simply being gender and race neutral, in a completely depoliticised model, had better effects. This approach has since taken centre stage in the theorisation of organisational diversity in business management sciences, creating an industry of consulting firms and professionals who often reinforce neoliberal ideologies across a broad range of specialities, including diversity, organisational psychology, and so on. 'Affirming diversity' as theory and praxis thus *instrumentalizes* and *managerializes* a movement that is supposed to be grounded in social and political aims: towards ensuring human rights, the protection of values such as equality and dignity, and social justice imperatives[56].

Merely 'affirming' diversity positions difference as an asset: as uniqueness, and innovation. Organisations using this approach may have quite nuanced and multi-pronged strategies, for example, applauding difference in their organisational cultures, while also giving attention to interpersonal relationships and building diverse teams to catalyse innovation and advance organisational effectiveness. However, it remains an apolitical approach that doesn't consider or question how systems work to reproduce privilege, and how its definition of 'difference' normalises what is already inside the company, i.e., in most contexts, the assumption of white, male, heterosexual superiority. Often this approach remains unconsciously compliant with this norm and doesn't go so far as to problematise some of its most basic assumptions. Because the organisation may appear to be 'inclusive' or even progressive, it can often be particularly difficult to challenge embedded patterns of exclusion or marginalisation.

4.1.3. Multiculturalism and Diversity Management

Around the turn of the last century, a conservative think tank called the Hudson Institute warned that in the 21st century labour market, about 85% of new entrants to the job market would be women and ethnic minorities, and that the decline of the

---

[54] For a discussion, and other aspects of this history, see Payne and Thakkar (2012).
[55] *From Affirmative Action to Affirming Diversity* (Thomas, 1990).
[56] For a detailed critique, see Litvin (2002).

"Baby Boomer" generation (mostly white men) in the workforce signalled the need for companies to start more assiduously "managing diversity". These projections were lent a sense of real urgency by McKinsey & Company's hypothesis that an ageing population and the retirement of white men would send companies into a "war for talent" where diversity would need to be placed at the epicentre of talent acquisition.

The research agenda set by these warnings produced studies that focused on topics such as the effects of diversity management on various dimensions of organisational performance, the increasing "border permeability" of talented workers, globalisation, and cross border trade, and technological advancement in the knowledge economy [57]. Multiculturalism became a central theme in diversity management practice and scholarship. The term "multiculturalism" which sounds as if it might signal a move towards a deeper commitment to diversity has in fact accompanied an ideology aimed at legitimising the assimilating ethnic diversity in the majoritarian (usually Anglophone) society, and a public policy designed to assimilate ethnic diversity into a culturally monolithic national unity[58]. While multiculturalism had some radical origins grounded in critical practices that need to be taken into account[59], much of its potential is reined in and cancelled out by managerialism.

Interventions in this space often focus on increasing awareness amongst staff about each other's cultural backgrounds. Differences between people are typically defined in terms of their ethnic and religious affiliations, with little or no reference to histories of racial and colonial oppression. The main message is that all cultures are to be treated equally, and that everyone should exercise tolerance and respect towards one another. When conflict or intolerance do occur, this is most often attributed to individual ignorance or cultural misunderstanding, rather than to power dynamics rooted in unfair histories. Multiculturalism in a diversity management paradigm is also often associated with problematic cultural reductionism about which groups are 'good at' certain tasks. Who can read maps and who has no sense of direction; who will look you straight in the eye and who will study the floor; who is a computer or financial guru and who is more of a people person: all of these simplistic, often racist stereotypes are potentially brought to the surface and even reproduced in a multicultural paradigm that sees cultural difference as an exploitable 'asset' for an organisation.

Sending staff for "cultural sensitivity training" or devising special days or events to "celebrate" different cultures are indicative of this kind of multicultural approach. Managing diversity supposedly aims to increase an organisation's competitive edge while at the same time using the 'melting pot' image as a way to enforce a uniform corporate culture, affirming the idea that "we are all the same underneath" as long as

---

[57] See Gwele (2009), Hoch, Pearce and Welzel (2010), Jayne and Dipboye (2004), and Kundu (2003) for examples of this kind of research from around the world.

[58] See Bekker and Leildé (2003) for analysis of this concept in the South African context.

[59] For a discussion, see Shohat and Stam (2014).

we adhere to our brand values! The organisation often promotes awareness of how decisions may be negatively affected by stereotypes and prejudice and how this in turn may undermine team effectiveness, productivity and profitability. The primary motivation for this approach is that it makes good business sense to 'manage' diversity, as opposed to it being a legal obligation, or a moral or political imperative. The implicit assumption is that without sound management, diversity could get out of control or lead to conflict or underperformance. Interventions under this approach typically have a strategic emphasis on finding common ground and are often aimed at managers as the primary agents of making diversity 'work' as an asset for the organisation.

4.1.4. The Psycho-Social Paradigm

Psycho-social theorists tend to focus on minimising the possible counterproductive effects of diversity. As a result, scholars associate increased organisational diversity with negative outcomes such as interpersonal conflict, communication inefficiencies, absenteeism, presenteeism (being present at work but not productive) and high voluntary turnover of minority groups [60] . These scholars, who tend to be organisational behaviour and industrial psychologists, apply social identity and self-categorisation theories to examine the intra- and intergroup dynamics in a heterogenous work context.

Social identity and self-categorisation theories are interconnected social psychology theories that explain the intrinsic human need for belonging, and the human propensity to organise based on perceived identity similarities. In-group similarities and out-group differences are often exaggerated. This results in the conception of stereotypes and the depersonalisation of an individual in order to fit into the stereotype. In-groups thus tend to establish normative behaviours that smooth out their own social interactions, while out-groups are characterised as deserving of hostility, marginalisation, and rejection based on their non-normative identity and behaviours. Extensive research in this space has shown how (intra-company) ethnic and racial minorities, as well as LGBTI workers, struggle to find coaches and mentors, for example.

This approach can inappropriately pathologize discrimination within the workplace, and inadvertently reify social norms as being hardwired into people's brains: it's not their fault, it's just human psychology. Psychological theories have been instrumentalised as management tools in the forms of psychometric tests, which form part of an array of assessment instruments that have subsequently been developed to profile a job applicant's propensity to "fit in" within the existing dominant culture. Once again, history, power, and culture are absent from the analysis.

---

[60] For examples of this kind of research, see Milliken and Martins (1996) and Pelled (1996).

4.1.5. The Generational Socialisation Hypothesis

Some scholars within management sciences are increasingly framing diversity as a matter of different eras of socialization within an intergenerational workforce. This discourse argues that human differences are understood differently, and result differently in conflict, mistrust, and inequality, based on which generation team members belong to. The socialisation hypothesis has developed in tandem with so-called "generational theory" and the idea that social change may be linked to "cohorts' of people that grow up in similar times and spaces[61]. One's generational 'location' is understood to indicate some definitive modes of behaviours, feelings and thoughts. These are understood as being linked to the social and material conditions that shape the adult's values through the socialisation process, and that the experiences they might have had in their youth of different levels of economic and physical security have instilled enduring value orientations.

Despite being highly criticised for conceptual flaws and theoretical as well as empirical inconsistencies[62] the generational socialisation theory is flourishing in management discourse. Generational theorists differ substantially in their description of generational cohorts, the socio-historical events, and timelines that shape and differentiate generational cohorts, and fail to account for geo-political, socio-cultural and economic nuances in various contexts. Popular names for the generations the Silent Generation, the Boom Generation, Baby Boomers, Gen Xers, and Millennials, and even Post Millennials are highly contested even within the narrow geographical and social domains within which they can be said to have any purchase. Diversity within the organisations becomes a matter of waiting for the right set of generational attitudes to come along Millennials, for example, are said to deal better with diversity than Baby Boomers rather than being a matter of social change that is urgent in the present. Subject locations are theorised as being stuck in a particular period of socialisation, muddying notions of responsibility for making change happen.

In the South African context, pre-apartheid, early apartheid, grand apartheid, the Struggle, and the "Born Free" generations all co-exist within post-apartheid social life[63]. Theorising their impact on the workplace however involves over-simplistic generalisations, and many of the predictions about the impact of various groups on the social fabric have not been borne out in reality. Ultimately, generational socialisation is too blunt, reductive, and broad a tool to amply account for the nuances of difference within organisational life.

---

[61] The development of these ideas are most closely associated with Mannheim (1952), and Ryder (1965) and entered into management science in the 1990s (see Inglehart, 1990; Inglehart & Welzel, 2010).
[62] See Brooks and Manza (1994), Butler and Savage (2013), and Tilley (2005).
[63] See Mattes (2012).

4.1.6. The Inclusion Paradigm

'Inclusion' has recently emerged as a discourse that responds to diversity management's failure to successfully integrate diverse groups into the workplace. Proponents of this paradigm argue that the objective of inclusion discourse is to promote the creation of empowering organisational environments of differences in which diverse groups feel included and connected[64]. This approach is associated with pluralism and with "salad bowl" conceptualisation of diversity. Emphasis is placed on transcending the assimilationist melting pot concept to address issues of acceptance, appreciation, utilisation and celebration of similarities and differences at personal, interpersonal, systemic or institutional and cultural level. However, some scholars question whether inclusion is just "old wine" i.e., the old affirming diversity, or multicultural models, in a "new bottle"[65]. Much of the theoretical and practical apparatus associated with inclusion indeed seems to lead down previous dead ends.

'Inclusion' has suffered from inconsistent definitions. Some consider it to refer to whether employees are accepted and treated as insiders, others have focused it on the removal of barriers. All too often, both barriers and acceptance are not historicised and linked to their broader socio-political contexts.

4.1.7. The Corporate Social Responsibility Paradigm

The corporate social responsibility (CSR) paradigm recognises the power and impact of corporations on society. Businesses are understood to be called on to pursue policies, decisions and actions that are in alignment with social values and responsibility. This paradigm acknowledges to a very limited extent the role that corporations played in colonialism, slavery, and other forms of exploitation, and seeks to inculcate a culture of social consciousness in corporate pursuit of profits. The CSR model classifies corporate social performance in four dimensions: economic, legal, ethical and discretionary/philanthropic[66]. While some scholars in this domain view CSR as a tacit social contract between the corporation and society, and that the contract bestows certain rights and responsibilities to the organisation, others focus on an organisation's responsibility to the interests of specific stakeholders, where stakeholders are defined as any group or individual who can affect or is affected by the achievement of an organisation's purpose[67].

---

[64] See Bilimoria, Joy and Liang (2008) and Roberson (2006), and Roberson and Stevens (2006) for examples of this kind of perspective in action.

[65] This is Stella Nkomo's argument in an important chapter of *Diversity at Work: The Practice of Inclusion* (2014).

[66] Though these four dimensions have recently become fashionable, they were actually suggested by Sethi (1975) some time ago.

[67] See Donaldson (1982) and Donaldson and Dunfee (1999) for classic statements of the former position and Freeman (2010) for the stakeholder approach.

The CSR perspective frames diversity within a moral responsibility perspective, and tends to focus on corporate obligations towards labour, the environment, human rights, and poverty alleviation. Central to this paradigm is securing corporate profitability without neglecting the needs of society. Various international structures have been put in place to monitor corporate responsibility towards their social contexts. This perspective is linked to the notion of corporate citizenship behaviour, a concept that is grounded in the individual liberty, rights and responsibilities of the corporate as an individual citizen.

4.2.   Critiquing Managerial Instrumentalism

While the CSR perspective presents in certain senses an advance on other paradigms, as a model for diversity management it still does not offer tools for a substantial critique of the critical issues of power, inequality and social justice. Indeed, all seven of the diversity models we have considered above fall short of addressing real social problems in their appropriate historical contexts. This is largely because they are constructed within a broader paradigm: managerial instrumentalism.

As long as diversity falls within this management paradigm there is the danger that it represents nothing more than "colourful window dressing" [68]. Diversity management tactics often disregard critical questions of inequality, promote the assimilation of minority groups into dominant cultures without accounting for issues of hegemony, subjugation, and institutional prejudice, and serve as nothing more than "quick fixes" [69].

The search for the "business case" for diversity is common to all approaches under managerial instrumentalism. The logic of the business case is that some kind of bottom line benefit has to be shown in order for 'diversity' to be taken seriously by an organisation as a potential asset to be exploited, or as a risk to be minimised. A great deal of research has however failed to come up with a clear "business case" for diversity interventions within the current paradigms; studies in America have in fact suggested that businesses lose a significant amount of money every year, with little return for their investments [70].

Scholars have tried to prove that diversity has a positive impact on the profitability of a company, or on other aspects of performance, but have generally failed to do so conclusively. The problem quite clearly is in trying to bracket out other aspects of performance in a world where markets are seen as the ultimate arbiters of what is valuable. There is a sense in which this entire logic is self-defeating: if companies only care about diversity when it is profitable, they do not actually care

---

[68] See Marques (2010).
[69] See Noon (2007) and Cilliers and Stone (2005)
[70] It might be as much as $8-billion per annum in the United States (Hansen, 2003) or as much as $64-billion (Korn / Ferry Institute, 2007) with very little impact on the reasons people actually leave companies.

about diversity at all. It is only when social justice, real inclusion, and a progressive form of the social contract is valued for its *own* sake that managerial instrumentalism can be surpassed as the hypocritical approach that it is.

4.3.   Conclusion

For organisations to truly engage in social change, they will create opportunities to analyse power and oppression inside and outside of the organisation as an end in itself. In this way, organisations may keep themselves open and alert to authentic social change. In this scenario, the organisation becomes willing to redesign what it is and how it operates at the level of personal attitudes, institutional structures and the culture of the organisation as a whole. Leaders may draw on all of the approaches above, and take cognisance of cultural dynamics, accept the need for legal compliance, recognise the impact of diversity on organisational effectiveness, while also being committed to healing past wounds and learning about multiple expressions of difference. There is a profound and urgent need to surpass managerial instrumentalist approaches to difference in organisations. Interventions with a more critical approach are likely to be organic, bottom-up, self-organising, disruptive and unpredictable, and we will now turn to a discussion of their theoretical premises and principles.

Chapter 5

Getting 'Critical' About Diversity Literacy

Increasingly, scholarship has turned a critical eye on attempts within management sciences to accomplish a meaningful response to human diversity in organisational life within the framework of managerial instrumentalism[71]. *Critical* diversity scholars tend to draw from Marxist and post-Marxist critiques of capitalism, from the critical theory perspectives of the Frankfurt School, from feminist and post-/de-colonial theory, and other perspectives that theorise the link between diversity in capitalist corporations and the histories of slavery, coloniality, and the commodification of labour in late modernity.

While the diversity paradigms outlined in the previous chapter are hardly radical in their approach to organisational life, they do speak to shifts in the way that society is imagined[72]. It is clear that part of the problem organisations face is that they are trying to manage the *intrusion* of the social into their space, not understanding that their space has always been profoundly social, and that what is needed is not better business administration, but better social science. Critical and post-/de-colonial scholars have worked for decades to provide a comprehensive framework for conceptualising the interconnected dimensions of power, privilege, and oppression that historically and presently work together to sustain inequality in organisations as much as in any other sphere of public life. It is such an approach that we will present in this chapter.

5.1.   The Ten Principles of Critical Diversity Literacy

The interest of the critical diversity research stream is to identify, challenge and change hegemonic systems and processes of power that perpetuate oppression and domination in organisations. This scholarly tradition does not study race, gender, and class in their organisational context merely for theoretical purposes, or in order to increase the effectiveness of organisations, but with a genuine desire to promote social change. It is thus both a scholarly endeavour and an activist tradition.

Melissa Steyn's programme of action for critical diversity was inspired by the notion of racial literacy developed by the critical race theorist France Winndance

---

[71] Examples of more critical approaches to diversity in the workplace include work of Joan Acker (2004, 2006), Sara Ahmed (2007, 2012; Ahmed & Swan, 2006), and Stella Nkomo (e.g. 1992, 2007; 2011).
[72] See Vertovec (2012).

Twine in the context of the United Kingdom[73]. The notion of the need to develop 'literacy' can be applied to a range of social differences in addition to race, and expanded to include insights from feminist theory, critical race theory, critical disability theory, and queer theory[74]. The result is seeing an approach to all human diversity through a critical lens as being a kind of reading practice, termed Critical Diversity Literacy (CDL).

CDL is a ten-point distillation of a rich theoretical tradition that outlines the analytical skills required for a conscious and just engagement with human diversity. The approach does not envision that any single person is likely to be equally or fully adept at all the criteria. Rather, they should serve as avenues for on-going personal and professional development, both for diversity practitioners and for humanity at large. It can take a lifetime's work to become fully critically diversity 'literate' in this sense. In the organisational context, some simple pointers and measurements are required that do not require any specialised knowledge of critical theory. For this reason, it is necessary to start with a basic structure of how these skills, or lack of them, impact on the life of an organisation.

5.1.1. Power is the Difference that Makes a Difference

Differences between people are not actually that noteworthy in an organisational context unless they are made to matter in unequal power relations. The point about studying difference in the first place is that some people will benefit, while others will be disadvantaged by the difference. What might commonly be understood to be *natural* differences between people should always be analysed in terms of how what is supposedly 'natural' serves a particular power interest, assigning dominant and subordinate places to different groups in a hierarchical order. What is 'natural' is always and everywhere uncovered as the effects of how a dominant group has been able to manipulate social arrangements to their own advantage.

What some people are 'good' at, and others not, is an excellent example of how power has worked to create hierarchies. Take the 'STEM'[75] disciplines as an example: many of the people who work in these disciplines are men, who also tend to subscribe to a worldview that has a rather uncomplicated relationship with the notion of 'evidence'. The preponderance of men in STEM disciplines is seen as being 'evidence' that men are just more interested in, just more disposed to, and ultimately just better at science, technology, engineering, and mathematics. The truth is that this is an impossible conclusion: the historical and social development of STEM has been

---

[73] Steyn (2005). See Twine's important book *A White Side of Black Britain: Interracial Intimacy and Racial Literacy* (2010).
[74] The intellectual forebears of Critical Diversity Literacy are outlined in Steyn (2015). A good place to start for queer theoretical perspectives on management theory is Parker (2001); for an introduction to important concepts in critical disability theory, see Pothier and Devlin (2006).
[75] Science, Technology, Engineering, Mathematics

profoundly patriarchal, and it is illogical to conclude that innate ability cleaves to gender. The few examples of the women who excelled despite male domination Ada Lovelace, Marie Curie, or Katherine Johnson are not exceptions to the rule of natural male talent, but evidence of how hard it is for something as seemingly all-powerful and universal as the patriarchy to keep all women down at once.

Analysing the role that power plays in making differences means always being sceptical of hierarchies between people that are regarded as 'natural'. This requires interrogating how relations of power construct the difference in the first place, and how the maintenance of this construction serves those who already have power. The other nine principles of CDL are all linked to this fundamental insight.

5.1.2. Social Location Matters

Generally, people in dominant groups tend not to have the same levels of insight as those who are members of oppressed groups into how the systems of domination from which they are benefiting operate. The privileged are often insensitive to how oppressed people are impacted. People in dominated positions often have much more awareness of how unfairness is structured into the system, and that merit does not get them the same mileage, even if they work hard. However, they may also internalise their oppression, and come to share the understandings that they deserve to be where they are in the hierarchy.

As people, we tend to internalise a sense of our inferiority or superiority, because we attribute the things we have attained in life to what we *deserve*. Social justice militates against putting up with what we have in life as the just distribution and demanding instead that we ask deeper questions of why the goods of the world are distributed so unevenly.

Apologists for colonialism, for example [76], are usually also in some way its beneficiaries, and often write from positions of immense social and historical power, where their analysis is unchallenged by any daily lived realities. There is a fundamental subjectivity to our experiences that we need to take into account when thinking about difference: we can sympathise with what other groups experience, and imagine what it must be like to be them, but at the end of the day we can never really go through the same knowledge formation processes, share other people's experiences of reality, or partake of their collective and personal self-understandings. People do not make meaning within a vacuum: we speak from bodies that come with histories of domination and oppression, in specific social contexts [77]. The point of this is not that

---

[76] Such as the conservative Oxford and Harvard historian Niall Ferguson, who argues that Britain's colonies enjoy significant advances in medicine, infrastructure, and the advantage of proficiency in the global lingua franca, English.

[77] Inhabiting different social locations means that while it is important to build political alliances between groups with different histories and experiences, it is profoundly problematic to want to speak on behalf of other groups whose own voices must be heard in the fight for social justice (see Alcoff, 1991).

alliances between people are impossible but rather that working across social locations requires listening to what other people have to say and taking them seriously when they describe their experiences.

5.1.3. Oppressive Structures Overlap and Intersect

Because the system has been built around privileging a particular positionality, all the hierarchical orders whiteness, patriarchy, able-bodiedness, etc. are interconnected, working together to maintain the status quo. People who are disadvantaged in one dimension may attempt to maximise their advantage along other dimensions, even if it means pushing others down. Black feminists in the 1980s in the United States observed that they were marginalised both by Black men in the anti-racism movement, and by white women in the feminist movement[78]. In this case, blackness and womanhood *intersect* to produce a positionality that is more than just the sum of its parts.

Intersections may work together as "controlling images"[79] that bring together race, class, gender, sexuality, and ability into specific character sketches African American women are "welfare queens"[80]; 'Coloured' men in South Africa are "gangsters". CDL entails being able to unpack intersecting systems of oppression to see how they are reproduced, negotiated, and how they may be deconstructed. While these systems are durable, they are also contingent on historical developments, and may be resisted and reframed.

5.1.4. Focus on Oppression as Present

In his campaign for the US presidency, Barack Obama famously quoted a line from William Faulkner: "The past isn't dead. It isn't even past." Whatever one might feel about Obama's ability once president to deal with the past in the present, it is clear that a particular narrative about oppression seeks to situate *real* oppression as something that happened a very long time ago, and the present as a triumph of democratic values and legal equality.

For CDL, it is important to take the past seriously in order to understand the dynamics that inform our present. The oppressive systems of modernity are not remnants of a past that we can simply forget. Racism, sexism, homophobia, disability, discrimination etc. are all operating integrally to the current system, and do not

---

[78] The classic texts from this period were written by the critical legal scholar, Kimberlé Crenshaw (1989, 1991). See Yuval-Davis (2006b) for a recent discussion of intersectional politics, and Collins (2015) for a discussion of the appropriate definition of the term 'intersectionality'.

[79] This term was developed by Patricia Hill Collins to describe the way that the hierarchies operate through constructing 'types' of people that are reproduced in human social life (2004).

[80] See Ruth Wilson Gilmore's (2007) classic analysis of controlling images and 'carceral Keynsianism' in the Californian prison system.

disappear by simply being declared irrelevant. We need to raise their operations to the level of consciousness and address them directly and systematically.

This is partly what is meant by the idea that the status quo must be appropriately *historicised*: it is in examining how a particular structure came to have its power over people that we can work towards changing it. Apologists for oppression will attempt to *naturalise* oppression: to make it seem like it has always been like this, in every human community. These arguments usually fail on two levels. On the first: there are almost always other times or cultures that did things differently. And as for the second: just because something is done in a particular way does not mean it ought to be done that way in future. There are countless places where human moral development diverges from claims about what is 'natural'.

Fundamentally, though, claiming the "past is past" is a diversion tactic that must be resisted. It is usually a claim made from social locations on whom the past does not reflect well: from the perspective of the historically oppressive. Facing up to the past is a necessary dimension of dealing with oppression in the present.

5.1.5.   Understanding that Social Identities are Learned

The world of meanings that we live in as human beings, our shared reality, is built by us collectively. Our sense of ourselves develops within this world of sociality. We cannot attribute characteristics to groups of people as if these are eternal, essential and unchanging. This type of stereotyping in the controlling images discussed above is a mechanism of power, used to fix people in a stratified relation to other groups. Because the stratification develops over time to benefit some while harming others, there are different stakes for different people in deconstructing these systems of identities.

Power normalises social identities through creating a sense that there is something essentially (biologically or culturally) different about a particular group of people that we have no social control over. These stereotypes mask the socially constructed and contingent nature of all social identities. Most insidiously, and importantly for CDL, is the phenomenon of members of oppressed groups who actively participate in the maintenance of oppressive systems. This *learned oppression* means that just knowing a person's social location is not enough to assume that their analysis of the system or of their own implication in it is beyond critique or question. CDL requires opening up the space for dialogue and dissent around not only how the Other is constructed, but also around how we construct our senses of Self.

5.1.6.   Learning Another Language

An important part of being competent in a heterogeneous world characterised by mutuality and respect, rather than domination, is developing a language to talk about our differences the power dynamics, the sensitive issues, the fraught experiences in ways that are both respectful, and analytically useful. We need to learn the vocabularies of respect; at the same time as unlearning what many of us have been taught is the 'normal' way to talk about difference. For many people, it is normal to talk about the "opposite" sex, about two genders, or to fixate on whether a new-born baby is a 'boy' or a 'girl' and to buy blue gifts for the boys and pink gifts for the girls, in line with western colour associations. This is part of an oppressive language that needs to be unlearned. Transgender, gender-fluid, and genderqueer people are challenging society to develop a new way of talking about gender, a way that does not systematically erase their experiences or erode their legitimacy as human beings. Systems that force people into choosing one of only two pronouns, or that insists on addressing people in a ways that does not reflect their gender identity, are signs of a society that is failing to educate itself about gender, and to develop the necessary vocabulary to talk about it.

Furthermore, being able to name the dynamics of oppression is an important first step to being able to challenge them; diversity vocabulary and grammar allows a challenging of 'folk' theories of difference, and the introduction of more sophisticated and challenging conversations. Very often, there is power at work in what may be named and what must remain unnamed. Disciplinary social power is often accompanied by technologies of shame, specifically around aspects of identity such as sexuality. Being able to name your own experiences and desires (as opposed to having them named for you) can very often be a first step towards reducing shame. Taking ownership of producing vocabulary and working against top-down modes of analysis that medicalise or marginalise particular dimensions of human difference, has been an important tactic in many struggles for equality.

Naming is of course just one dimension: the language that is built with CDL goes hand-in-hand with a deeper analytical practice, one that seeks to unmask oppressive power relations in our everyday personal and organisational lives.

5.1.7.   Decoding Oppression

Developing the language to analyse oppressive power enables an analytic capability that identifies the way that harmful social structures manifest themselves in the world. Power does not name itself as such; it is typically neither bare nor overt, and draws on common, implicit assumptions, attitudes and beliefs that are understood as referring to something beyond what is immediately apparent: something sensible, something eternal.

A good example of this is managerial talk about 'merit' and 'standards'. In conversations about affirmative action, for example, it might become normal for people to casually start using 'on merit' to mean 'not on the basis of equal opportunity policy'. This casual slippage can easily come to encode notions of racial superiority or inferiority, especially when what is being implied is that a white candidate gets a job/promotion on the basis of merit, whereas the Black employee will only ever get it on the basis of policy interference. A similar type of code is involved in traditional liberal assertions of 'open opportunity society' with 'level playing fields' which very often merely encode the idea that privileged white people should face no obstacles in being able to reproduce their existing positions in society far into the future.

5.1.8. The Material Matters

It may seem that the emphasis on social construction neglects the importance of economic, spatial and other material relations. This principle of CDL, however, goes to the heart of some of rich sociological debates on how human social life (our *cultures*, and the way we make meaning) interacts with the material affordances of our existence (the lived realities of our daily work and lives, our household economies, how well fed, clothed, and housed we are) and how these affordances constitute the *structures* of our lives. We analyse these as being in a dialectic relationship with each other i.e., richly co-constructing and mutually determining each other that is also interpenetrative, i.e., it is hard to say where the one stops and the other begins.

If we take the example of the patriarchal order, it is clear that different *cultural* expressions of patriarchy, or patriarchies, can be found all over the globe. While all of these may subordinate women, they play out in different arrangements in different contexts, using different language, different forms of bodily discipline, different economic arrangements i.e., they are also *structured* differently. They co-construct each other when, for example, a woman's financial dependence on a man is used to justify his higher salary, while the acceptance of the higher value of men's labour in the workplace condones at a cultural level keeping women in dependent, homebound in 'free' labour relations to men. Men are allowed to dominate businesses because their labour is valued more highly, and their labour is valued more highly precisely because they are allowed to dominate the business world.

The interdependence of culture and structure is everywhere apparent: Why are disabled children placed in faraway, special schools in some societies, out of sight and out of mind? Why are so many public amenities designed with able-bodied people in mind? Is it because physical disability is so uncommon[81] or is it simply because able-bodied chauvinism has been allowed unchecked to structure public space that should belong to all of us? Space, social context, history, and material arrangements are in dynamic relationships with social constructions. The work of CDL is also the work of unpicking these relationships.

5.1.9. Emotions Perform Social Labour

While we tend to think of emotions as purely individual, they are in fact very much shaped by, and shapers of, our social world. We are taught whom to respect, whom to

---

[81] It's not at all. See Mont (2007).

hold in contempt, whom to fear, whom to trust etc., and it is the circulation of these emotions that helps to create and maintain the boundaries along which inclusion and exclusion happen[82]. The important thing is for each of us not only to recognise these patterns in social relations, but also to develop self-reflexivity to understand our own emotional investments: if we feel defensive, what are we protecting? Why are we angry when some topics are raised, and indifferent to others?

Much of the Eurocentric Enlightenment's focus was on drawing clear distinctions between reason and passion, with the passions assigned inferior roles when it comes to the progress of human knowledge. Passion was constructed as a feminine, savage, uncivilised thing that might be good for creating Romantic art but had no place in the advance of science. Rather than banishing emotions, this tradition really only served to mask a particular way of looking at the world, as emotional as any other, but labelled it "dispassionate" and rational and associated it with white men.

The analysis of affect in CDL is as much about the importance of unmasking supposedly 'dispassionate' versions of the world as biased and anything but unemotional, and in observing the structuring role that the cohesive and adhesive forces of emotion play in creating in- and out-groups, in preventing the development of new vocabularies, in discounting the experiences of others, and so on. Emotions cannot and ought not to be banished from the analysis of social inequalities; they must be engaged with meaningfully.

5.1.10. A Commitment to Social Justice

In the end, the rearrangement of relations between groups of people is about developing a different ethic. An important principle is mutual recognition: people need to be heard, to know that their contribution to society is valued, that they are safe, and that they matter. Mutual understandings of what these principles amount to in specific contexts need to be negotiated.

While the first principle of CDL underpins the other nine, this final principle is the necessary personal enactment of all the preceding ones: if you develop the skills and practices listed above, a commitment to social justice emerges. Being critically literate implies taking action in the real world to change relations of domination and inequality.

We cannot deal with the new realities of the world with old mindsets. The full plurality of humanity can co-exist in the same space; difference cannot be 'managed' away, nor can it be outsourced. To try to deal with difference through domination is a recipe for conflict: it invites the counter thrust; it spawns challenge. On the other hand, minding one's own business is also not a solution. Receding into 'tribal' responses that seek comfort in familiarity in the midst of heterogeneity narrow down

---

[82] See Sara Ahmed's (2001, 2004) important work on how emotions circulate as "affective economies" that work politically to determine who is loved, and who is hated.

one's cultural space, seeking ways to regroup or recreate a sense of homogeneity, based on a nostalgia for times when things seemed to be simpler. Those times are simply not coming back. We need to develop mindsets and skills that support living together in much more mutual ways. This is the direction that has the weight of historical fact.

Learning to be diversity literate is a lifelong learning process. But if we want to be qualified for leadership in the world as it is unfolding, we do not really have the luxury of deciding whether we feel like taking on this line of personal growth or not.

5.2.   Critical Diversity Literacy as a Reading Practice

What is CDL actually? Is it a philosophy, is it a practice, is it a policy? At its core it is a reading practice that gives you critical skills to bring change. But what has to be in place to enable that change? Or does the change come after you've been exposed to a CDL process? Is it micro-skills that people learn in human relations? Is it an awareness that you have? Is it a set of values and principles? I think it's all of those things.

– Pierre Brouard

The language we use to talk about ourselves and our organisations is incredibly important. Language is the domain of visions and missions, sales pitches and value propositions, staff employment contracts and stakeholder agreements. It has been argued that all transformation occurs through language[83]. The words we choose, and what we take them to mean, are incredibly important to our social and organisational lives, and we therefore need to pay careful attention to them. This is not in any way to distract attention away from the imperatives of structural, tangible, economic change: of wealth and land transfer, of changes in ownership structure. The point, instead, is to highlight how these material imperatives are contested discursively.

In South Africa, businesses have tended to talk about the imperative for post-apartheid racial and social change as 'transformation'. The word 'transformation' comes with its own baggage, not least of which is its association with the mixed success of organisational change mentioned above, which has seen nearly 70% of top management positions still go to white people nearly a quarter of a century since the end of apartheid. So part of the work of 'transformation' today must mean opening up what transformation means or *could possibly mean* opening up the possibility for change through removing the barriers to whatever keeps people from having the conversations and thus making the meaning, constructing the new social reality that

---

[83] This argument is developed by the business writer Peter Block in his book, *Community: The Structure of Belonging* (2008).

really matter. There is already a language field through which meetings and conversations take place. The vocabularies we share in these settings impact on who we are and what we do together. Certain words carry more power and currency. Concepts that are pushed forward and constantly reinforced stand a better chance of gaining acceptance. They become the new 'normal'. In organisational and social settings, there is a tacitly agreed way of talking about change that seems appropriate and doesn't rock the boat too much. Social norms within an organisation can create environments in which important things go unsaid, out of fear that if they are said a fragile peace will somehow be violated. And so while people grumble about 'political correctness' and 'snowflakes' who do not want to be offended, the real snowflakes are those who cannot see how their own views dominate and silence the perspectives of others.

This is one of the reasons why CDL interventions should avoid being structured as in-and-out consulting projects. Many practitioners prefer to think of the work of diversity as a form of coaching:

> *I did consulting for many years, going and telling, telling, telling, telling, and yes you can go in and convince people and you see the 'aha' moments. But I'm actually more and more convinced that a coaching model is what is needed and not a consulting model. Because with consulting you go in and you tell all the right things. And people will be with you and they'll say the right things, but will they actually change? I'm not so convinced. A coaching model says you must help them discover what's already present within them, what's already present within the system, that can lead them to change.*

> **– Jennie Tsekwa**

As an intervention, Critical Diversity Literacy fundamentally provides a common language for organisations to pursue diversity literacy. It is not a theory of business administration, or a model that may be shepherded through a standard organisational change process. The key to understanding what it is that CDL practitioners do in an organisation is this: they create the discursive conditions for people in the organisation to lead the change themselves.

5.3.   Conclusion

The ten principles of CDL together constitute the beginnings of a reading practice that enables people in organisations and in social life more generally to become conversant in human diversity in a way that dissolves harmful power structures, and the painful barriers between people. As such, it is a potentially world-changing approach. But before it can change the world, people have to be convinced that it is the correct course of action. For that reason, we will now examine one way to 'sell' a

CDL intervention to an organisation, so that expectations and ground rules are clear from the start.

Chapter 6

Why Should Organisations Choose CDL?
Selling CDL to Management

As CDL practitioners, we are often asked to become part of 'selling' the concept to organisations in ways that align with their particular business models. Unfortunately, we normally get approached when things are pretty broken already. Organisations are looking for quick fixes. We know that developing literacy is not a quick fix; but it is also the only fix that will stick. So the question to the head of an organisation should be: while you are doing it, why not do it properly?

When starting work with an organisation for the first time, one of the basic problems we often face is a misunderstanding both of the nature of the problems they have, and the nature of the service we offer. These both need to be clarified in the process of signing up a company and enrolling its leadership. The first impetus of this group is very often to deny that they really have a problem, and to describe people who have spoken up as trouble-causers in an otherwise harmonious unit.

These two basic things that there is a real problem, and that there is no quick fix can be hard for organisations to hear. Even more challenging, however, can be the philosophical fit between the organisation and the CDL practitioner. Most organisations are framed within the assumptions of capitalism and often do not question its current neo-liberal instantiation. The critical approaches to race, gender, disability, and sexuality, on the other hands, prioritise social justice.

So, what common ground can there possibly be between a CDL practitioner and a business leader, school headmaster, or the vice-chancellor of a neoliberal university? If we are committed to social equality in our work, then we will have to pay close attention to creating that common ground. It can seem like a real challenge to people to implement CDL. How on earth does one "sell" it? It is very far removed from standard management models, which rely on the stability of a particular commercial-corporate ideology when thinking about management and the definition of success. If not rejected as a crazy idea outright, CDL can be undermined as an ineffectively theoretical intervention, when what needs to happen is concrete action.

The battle between thinking and theorising on one hand, and doing on the other, requires a feat of translation. The language of critical theory and decolonial theory is of course *not* the language of everyday business administration, and we would be unsurprised to find executives failing to discuss the social construction of reality in their weekly meetings. So, if we do accept the ten points in Chapter 5, how do we translate these into real capacity within the organisation?

It is our theoretical starting point that the way that change, diversity, and transformation are spoken about within the organisation literally *constructs* these realities. If change is spoken about as a threat, it will always seem threatening within the organisation, until a discourse of opportunity is introduced. If CDL is conceived of as an existential threat to the organisation, then there are simply fewer reasons why anybody within the organisation should embrace it.

We will address this complex issue in five sections below. In §6.1 we orient CDL around organisational purpose. In §6.2 we articulate the philosophical framework of CDL in such a way that it clearly accommodates a variety of purposes. In §6.3 we make some suggestions for the integration of aspects of the language of CDL into the language of organisational management. In §6.4 we present the negative case for CDL: why not developing it harms businesses. Finally, in §6.5, we consider the question of whether some organisations are just so problematic that it becomes impossible to work in them.

6.1. Understanding Organisational Purpose

Organisations are often oriented around single-outcome grand narratives about their purpose. These high-level outputs are specific to sectors, for example:

- Businesses organise themselves around maximising profit to their shareholders.

- Non-profit organisations organise themselves around social impact and raising the funding to achieve it.

- Universities aim to improve their place in the global ranking system.

- Secondary schools tend to measure themselves in terms of their indicators such as (in the South African context) their matriculation pass rate.

This does not mean that these are the only indicators, of course. We are familiar with mines, for example, that target zero work-related injuries and deaths; these injuries and deaths do however occur, though the thing that will shut the mine down is when it becomes unprofitable to run it. Particular goals of the organisation its environmental impact, its staff development and safety, its social impact are very often subordinate to the notion of an overarching purpose. Organisations may have long lists of goals, but the high-level ones, the ones that impact most on their productivity and profitability "1.5-million tons of ore per day!" are frequently those that will be pinned up in boardrooms, and the focus of strategic and operational planning.

It is clear that a lack of CDL *may* impact negatively on these high-level indicators in all of these sectors, but this is not the whole story. One could argue that universities mired in conflict don't climb ranking tables, or that businesses with unhappy staff don't innovate to enhance their productivity. Still, the norm is that organisations can get away with it if they are sustained and supported in cultural bubbles that affirm their practices. For example, South African private schools that have mostly white learners and teachers are sustained and affirmed by parents and an education department keen on not alienating the School Governing Body; homophobic non-profit organisations are sustained by funders who pay to see 'Family Values' reproduced. So an alignment between 'success' and improved CDL can never be assumed.

The core value of CDL is that stratified social systems sustained by unequal power relations are harmful and unfair. They are *morally* reprehensible, first and foremost. To this we could add that they are also volatile and unstable in a rapidly changing world. While unfairness is wrong even if it happens behind closed doors, it is important to remember that these doors are increasingly being flung open. A commitment to dealing with difference in a way that challenges harmful social structures may not always be clearly aligned with the purpose of a particular organisation in the present, but this is an inherently fragile arrangement, protected only by the longevity of the cultural bubble in which it exists.

Another theme that is important to develop in our conversations with organisations (and one that is developed throughout this book) is that of *discomfort*. Improved CDL in an organisation is not going to sit comfortably inside of an operational plan as an affirming way to reach one or more company goals. Its effects will be to irritate and to agitate, because it is fundamentally an intervention to *change* the way that leadership operates. Melanie Judge puts this in a particularly acute way:

> *Some leaders feel, 'Why should I be interested in a substantive racial transformation in my organisation? Because it's going to change the way that I have to lead, it's going to change the culture of the organisation... Why should I be interested in substantive gender transformation, because it's going to change my capacity to make comments about women's bodies in the office!' There is a contradiction in trying to make leadership comfortable with change, because at the heart of this work is discomfort. Discomfort is the lubricant of critical diversity literacy. The minute the case is framed in such a way that it is too comfortable; it's doing something normative, and can work against the process itself.*

– Melanie Judge

This is a crucial insight for aligning the CDL process with organisational purpose. Because CDL is aligned with a moral imperative that affects all members of an organisation, and the communities linked to and affected by that organisation, it is likely to cause friction with the leadership orientation of the organisation. It is the job of the CDL practitioner to convince the leadership of the organisation that this friction is worth it: especially when it becomes uncomfortable for the leaders themselves who have commissioned the process. For both parties, this can seem a bit like "dancing with the devil". While it is not possible to rationalise away the discomfort that a CDL intervention will cause for the organisation and especially for its leadership, neither are CDL and pursuing the overarching goal mutually exclusive. Profitability, university ranking, organisational funding or school academic performance can exist alongside a commitment to internal social justice, and these commitments can be aligned to strengthen the organisation.

6.2.   What We Ask Companies to Accept

We have thus established that a CDL process is by definition uncomfortable, but that it does not need to represent an existential threat to the organisation. What other principles do we ask organisational leaders to accept in order for the CDL process to adequately take root in an organisation? We will examine five of them in this section: that organisations are continuous with the social world, that diversity crises are symptoms of deeper patterns of thinking, that the social world is exceptionally complex and hard to predict, that stakeholders very often hold the key to an improved organisation, and that individual organisations need not shy away from leading in the space of critical diversity literacy.

6.2.1.   Organisations are Part of the Social World

Organisations are not disconnected islands in a transparent ocean, nor are they insulated from the ravages of what happens to people, communities, nations, or continents. As we have already discussed, a social media campaign can sink a brand; a protest can shut down and then restructure a university; a new way of understanding identity can contribute significantly to staff disengagement. Organisations that think that "the social" or worse still "politics" stops at their front door, are self-deluding and vulnerable. We will look at some specific case studies when we assess the harm of low CDL in §6.4.

A crucial first step is to get the leadership of an organisation to agree that they are part of the social world, and that what happens in the community is also happening in the organisation. Poverty, inequality, homophobia, the patriarchy, and racism, are part of the fabric of the organisation because this very fabric is made up of people in society. It is not possible simply to screen out social problems in hiring practices, or in commitment to a particular corporate culture: social problems are organisational problems. The idea in dealing with them is to keep constantly connected and engaged with the people of the organisation.

But how do you enable that engagement? How do you bring people closer together, rather than pulling them apart? How do you decrease often radical polarisation? How do you talk about experiences that people have based on their identity locations, but without essentialising them? The courageous conversations that we will describe later on in this book are what we bring as CDL facilitators: it is our job to enable these dialogues, to build these skills. CDL is built through dialogue and conversation.

6.2.2. Your Current Crisis is Caused by Your Current Thinking

This is something of a management cliché, but it is still surprising that organisational leaders cannot see the connections between their own thinking, and the crisis of diversity in their organisations. They seek to externalise the problem to attribute the problem to factors outside of their control, rather than examining what they do control and how their manner of controlling has contributed to the crisis. If an organisation really is in crisis, this can be an excellent opportunity to introduce change.

As was discussed under the "social locations" principle of CDL, those who are most resistant to self-reflection and problematising of the social are most likely to themselves occupy powerful social locations, or to have benefited in some way from harmful social systems, even if they do not themselves inhabit *prima facie* powerful locations. It is commonly related from our practice that (for example) the lone woman in senior management will attribute her own success to hard work and the right kind of attitude, and describe women demanding better working conditions at lower levels as troublesome moaners. Black managers can participate in upholding a white supremacist corporate culture because they see their own success as proof of the fairness of the system, and it is hard to reconcile your own experience of being rewarded with other people's reports of structural unfairness.

From white managers we hear that "I am colour-blind, I don't see race" and that this is the end of the analysis. What a CDL practitioner must work to get the organisational leaders to accept is that no matter how blameless they think they are, they are still part of a problematic social system that needs to be spoken of in the open. The problems of diversity are not quickly rooted out by incentivising good behaviour and punishing bad; they subsist in deep structures that can rise to the surface in numerous and unanticipated ways. The only solution is to go right to the root of the problem in people's most deeply held beliefs, into the ideological structures of their own positions and personalities.

6.2.3. The Social World is Not Easily Predictable

Part of the work of a manager is to demand a specific, quantifiable deliverable within a certain timeframe. Management often consists in turning risks and opportunities into measurable benefits. Intervening in the social structures that underlie organisational life is however an intrinsically uncertain, unquantifiable undertaking. Add to this the platitude that we live in times of high uncertainty, and organisational leadership might well be concerned that they may have to abandon certainty altogether.

As was discussed in Chapter 4, the search for the definitive "business case" for diversity management did not produce a clear result, contributing to our decision to discard managerial instrumentalism as a framing assumption. The work of CDL is built on an ethical foundation, and not on projections of its profitability. CDL practitioners must therefore focus on unmasking the supposed certainty of a business case as an illusion. Illusions can be dangerous. Organisational leaders that want absolute certainty in managing social change wilfully prevent themselves from knowing the exact scope of their control.

What CDL offers is a conversation that better networks an organisation into what its internal and external communities think and feel about it, and each other. It offers people in leadership positions the opportunity to decide to stop working at cross-purposes to the self-determination of individuals and their communities. It offers a mode of responsiveness that feeds off the creativity of people, off the myriad solutions that arise in complex social systems. Pre-empting what these solutions will be can undermine the whole process.

6.2.4. Get More in Touch with Your Stakeholders, Not Less

Because social systems are complex and unpredictable, a responsible organisational leader will get more in touch with people, not less. And yet too many of the leaders we encounter in our work are doing their utmost to silence the voices of their stakeholders or hide community dissent from view. This is another dangerous, self-imposed illusion.

Because it is impossible for organisations to insulate themselves from social change, and the organisation already has access to people engaged within this social change within their own staff and other stakeholders, what is required from leadership is the humility to listen to what people are really saying. Increasingly, businesspeople are reaching a point where they say: we are businesspeople, we know how to make money, but we realise that something is not holding. We need to change the model. But how should the model be changed? The strategy has to come from the admission that no business exists in a vacuum. What many managers are taught in business school does not prepare them to listen. CDL does exactly this kind of preparation, helping organisations to become more connected internally and with their stakeholders.

> *I ask: in what ways can we learn to seek each other's best in a way that's good for us all? For me it translates into our models of the social, the economic and the political. So, I advocate for what I would call a relational wholeness, or connectedness. I challenge people to listen to their stakeholder perspectives rather than first reducing them to specific interests. All of the people who really have a stake in this organisation: how do our policies and procedures impact on them?*

I believe we can unlock the best in our human nature, if we can ask this question of more organisations.

– Kirsten Klopper

The separation of workers from bosses into blank class antagonism can be a self-fulfilling prophecy. Our approach is to get people working collectively without engaging in zero-sum tactics i.e., whatever I gain, you lose; whatever I lose, you gain. This is an unsustainable way for an organisation to operate. Organisations that wish to be adaptive and relevant, and that seek to align their internal operations with the 'external' social world, create some of the conditions of possibility for the success of CDL.

6.2.5. Leading in Your Own Space

Our societal failures, and the shortcomings of successive governments, have created a sense that our problems are intractable. A sense of dismay at sluggish performance in job creation, education, and general social uplift may already be built into the operating assumptions of organisations, who try to manage against their social reality, rather than face the challenging, even dispiriting, task of engaging with it.

Organisations also tend to look to their peers to competitor companies, to similarly ranked universities, to NGOs in the same space to see how they are responding to particular social challenges. Organisations worry that if they get distracted from a tenacious focus on their central purpose their profit or impact or ranking they will be overtaken by the competition and lose their relevance. The final thing the CDL practitioner therefore needs to convince organisational leaders of is that benchmarking against other organisations in a paradigm of competition is not that useful when it comes to issues of diversity. We need to encourage them to lead in their own space, and for the sake of their organisations.

Organisations face urgent diversity challenges in the present. The lack of clear leadership from competitors is no reason to hold back in terms of trying challenging new ways to orient organisations around human diversity. In fact, there is the potential for organisations to make listening to their employees part of their core value proposition, and ultimately a dimension of their ability to exert leadership. If they are not afraid of doing this in other contexts, why would they be so anxious when it comes to social change?

Pockets of excellence are possible, and societal leadership can be taken on by organisations that see the world differently. We have plenty of evidence from the past of schools, campaigns, universities and businesses that have shifted social norms for the better. Responsible leaders will not sit around waiting for other social actors to do something.

Because CDL is not a quick fix and is located in the social world of employees and stakeholders, the business case needs to be seen as a long-term social investment.

6.3.   Working with Existing Conceptual Frameworks

When business, society, and politics are not separated, when they can be seen as interrelated and interactive, we need to be able to engage with a wide variety of conceptual frameworks to bring about change. Increasingly, companies admit that paradigms need to shift away from making *profiting off society*, to *being sustainable in a society*. But a considerable amount of work still needs to be done in this space.

The ultimate goal of CDL is about equality and equity, and it pursues this goal because doing good is an end in and of itself. Some companies have started to accommodate other kinds of aims in their own frameworks by talking of a "triple bottom line" and of making "corporate social investment". There are good reasons to be sceptical of a lot of CSI, much of which is doesn't aim to shift structures, or to address the root causes of poverty. Often, CSI initiatives are seen as continuous with 'charity' models where staff are sent off on team-building days to volunteer on assigned projects. But no amount of painting school buildings is going to create equity.

Other companies talk of "conscious capitalism" or "capitalism with a conscience". Does this signal a shift away from exploitative relationships? Or is it just a way to whitewash continued exploitation, and preserve privilege and power? The proof of whether there is any conscience involved needs to come in the way that companies do business.

> *I've worked with a company where management said things like "If it weren't for us, then there wouldn't be any jobs in this town, so everyone should be glad because we've created 2,000 jobs". They gave themselves a licence to be so abusive, just because they expected townspeople to be grateful they had a job. And that is so sick, because it's so disguised in this social ethos of "uplifting the community"!*

– Haley McEwen

An organisation that is in a mutually respectful relationship with its workers and its community obviously does not use this kind of logic. At the end of the day, who would want to work for an organisation that frames its community contribution in terms of blackmail?

There are a variety of ways in which the existing conceptual frameworks of various sectors can be brought into conversation with CDL. The idea is that our approach is not necessarily incompatible with standard management jargon. Here are a few examples:

- **Staff engagement:** Many organisations focus on maximising staff engagement. An organisation that is undergoing diversity crises is likely also to have very high levels of disengagement. If the organisation is failing at addressing race, gender, sexuality, at promoting transformation and inclusivity, people won't be happy. And an unhappy workforce is not a good thing for any organisation.

- **Critical thinking:** Businesses, schools, universities, NGOs... all of them need critical thinkers in order to respond creatively to changes in their environments, to respond adaptively and effectively. CDL is clearly a part of the journey and the critical traditions in which our model is based promotes more nuanced and complex understanding of the contexts within which organisations operate.

- **Risk management:** Another good case for a CDL intervention in contemporary management jargon is in the various dimensions of strategic management especially risk management, but also stakeholder management. CDL allows organisations to "see around corners" by being far more intimately in touch with the needs and aspirations of the communities they serve.

Each organisation will have different priorities, and a different way of making sense of CDL within their context. It can also be important not to force your particular reading of the value of CDL onto an organisation, but to feel out instead why they are so interested in working with you.

> *My eyes have been so opened. So I would go into a company and think, this is a great technical group, they need to be convinced by stats and numbers about why diversity is valuable... No! In their heart of hearts it is the moral imperative that is most important: it's just the right thing to do. So now I think I should just come in with the tools and the skills to help them figure out what their reason is!*

> **– Jennie Tsekwa**

6.4. Measuring the Harm of Low CDL

Another way to 'sell' CDL to management that supplements the positive reasons we have already mentioned is to summarise the ways in which low CDL can impact on the ultimate purpose of the organisation. We've already listed the *symptoms* of the organisation that is not dealing with diversity appropriately in the first chapter. But these symptoms are not always "mission-critical" and might get pushed onto the fringes of an organisation's operations into the peripheral space often associated with human resources interventions. CDL works best when positioned as mission-critical and led by the leaders of the organisation. To position CDL in this way, anxiety about success may be helpful in making the case. The point that needs to come across clearly to leaders is that, left unchecked, a lack of literacy in diversity can have major *negative* impacts on the success of their organisations. We provide some extreme examples in each of the sections below, though it is important to remember that low CDL does not need to have extreme or dramatic effects in order for these to gnaw slowly at the heart of an organisation, and eventually rot it from the inside out or make it socially irrelevant.

6.4.1.   Reputation

Public Relations or reputation management has become one of the major areas of risk for companies unable to deal appropriately with a changing social world. Many companies only react to their own internal racism, transphobia, or ableism when they are exposed on social media. This exposure can have a significant negative impact on the value of the organisation's brand on their reputation in the world.

> *The Italian designers Domenico Dolce and Steffano Gabbana thought they were creating brand value for Dolce & Gabbana in their frequently incendiary and outrageously insensitive positions on a number of social issues[84]. In 2017, they even released a t-shirt emblazoned with the logo "Boycott Dolce & Gabbana" which retailed at a mere $245. Controversy was their brand position. It seems however that people do not always enjoy being insulted and ridiculed. In November 2018, ahead of the launch of a new line and a huge fashion show in China, which accounts for about a third of global fashion sales, they released a series of advertisements online. In these adverts, a stereotypical and archaic China is represented, with giggling Chinese women being 'instructed' in how to eat Italian foods. In one scene, a tube-shaped Italian pastry (a cannolo) is said to be "way too big for you, isn't it?". Playing on racist and sexist stereotypes, and brazenly advancing Italian nationalism, cost D&G dearly. Their show was cancelled, a plethora of online retailers stopped stocking their clothes, and it is estimated that they lost millions of dollars in this clumsy and insensitive stunt.*

In our work, however, what we have noticed is that the *internal reputation* of the company also suffers. When we are called in to deal with the fallout from a PR disaster caused by a corporate decision or the social media response to a particular staff statement, we very often find that what it does is to bring to the surface all of the internal concerns about diversity that have been jostling to be heard, from the staff

---

[84] See Tashjian (2018) for a full run-down on this crisis.

themselves. Suddenly, people are taking sides on the issue that's in the public eye: Should the guy have been disciplined or not? Was the response fair? And so on. Building CDL in an organisation helps team members to get ahead of these issues before they spill out and cause major damage.

6.4.2. Team Performance

Organisations that are not diversity literate frustrate, hold back, and ultimately harm their staff and other stakeholders. "Business as usual" is not going to cut it especially in highly fractious and fast-changing societies like South Africa (although this applies to most of the world at the moment). People might not yet be articulating things in these terms, but often the bulk of the human capital within an organisation is already not being that effective for some reason or another: Not engaged, not creative, not part of the solution.

A sexist work environment is a hotbed of harassment and sexual violence. A racist work environment exposes people to a wide range of aggressive behaviours every day. The energy of these people is drained; their very existence is challenged in the simple act of arriving at work in the morning. Organisations will not benefit from their talents.

> *The successful 'disruptive' ride-hailing company Uber has had serious problems in attracting and retaining women to work for them. The reason seems to be a thoroughgoing macho culture, which has landed them in hot water on a number of occasions[85]. These include advertising a service in France where you could book "an incredibly hot chick" to be your driver, and a series of gaffes by the company CEO who at one point joked to GQ magazine that you should be able to use their app for a woman-on-demand service they would call "Boob-er". Their internal masculinist culture (as well as a number of other problems) manifested in a culture of impunity for sexual harassment, which eventually took a number of whistle-blowers (including Susan Fowler[86]) to expose. Fowler describes an internal work environment of fear and nausea, and even being driven to suicidal thoughts, where many women just wanted to escape their toxic work environment. This culture, and the reports that have exposed it, are still impacting negatively on Uber, and its ability to recruit new team members.*

---

[85] You can read some of the descriptions of these problems in Inc magazine (Raymundo, 2014).
[86] Read the exposé in The Verge: "To expose sexism at Uber, Susan Fowler blew up her life" (Lopatto, 2020)

Staff that are not valued, or who feel they cannot be themselves at work, will become passive or active resistors of progress within teams. Valued staff will leave. Many of the companies we work with will point to positive exit interviews (if exit interviews are conducted at all) to argue that they have left on good terms: but perhaps they are just smart enough to know that they shouldn't burn their bridges. If organisations want to know what their track record is really like in terms of retaining a diverse talent pool, they should look at their numbers, and ask themselves difficult questions about why women, or Black people, or disabled people, are unwilling to stay working for them for that long.

6.4.3.   Crisis with a Bang!

Diversity crises high profile discrimination cases, sexual harassment at work, or a big PR scandal can send organisations into organic crises that spread in unanticipated directions. Stakeholders flee. The funders of NGOs that have been exposed for covering up sexual harassment have stopped funding these NGOs; abusive schools have closed down; entire firms have ceased to exist because of their dodgy business practices. Issues linked to appropriate diversity practices can sink what may be seen as a viable brand, or significantly dent the bottom line in unpredictable ways. This is one of the key reasons why CDL needs to be seen as mission-critical by leadership.

> *In early September 2020 a number of users on Twitter, including Miss Universe Zozibini Tunzi, started sharing an ad they had seen on the website of the popular South African pharmacy and cosmetics chain Clicks. The ad was for the Unilever shampoo brand TRESemmé and featured four pictures of women and their hair. While the white, blond woman's hair was captioned as "fine & flat" and as "normal" the Black woman's hair was called "frizzy & dull" as well as "dry & damaged". A basic critical literacy could have decoded the racialized problems with this ad before it was sent out[87]. And yet initially Clicks' response was to blame the 'foreign' Unilever brand for the content, which they claimed had been posted directly to the site without their own intervention. The crisis was swift and decisive: activists (spearheaded by the Economic Freedom Fighters) ensured that Clicks stores around South Africa were unable to open. Within one week, the company announced that they had accepted the resignation of the executive responsible for letting the campaign through, and that TRESemmé products would no longer be stocked by Clicks. So while Clicks was able to weather the storm, TRESemmé did not.*

---

[87] See the analysis by Zimitri Erasmus (2000) of South Africa's "Hair Politics."

6.4.4. Irrelevance with a Whimper

Organisations do not always go out with a bang they can also go out with a whimper, as they slowly lose their relevance, losing touch with their stakeholders, eroding their market share, losing their best people, abandoning their institutional knowledge. When the creativity of the team is at a low ebb because people are not really valued and included in the workplace, there is no corrective force to bring the organisation back into relevance, nobody to solve the daily problems that come up, and nobody to look over the horizon to the next big challenge.

There are examples of these flailing organisations all around us: though what would ultimately be blamed for their demise might not be low CDL, but a lack of support by their stakeholders. Customers stop buying, managers stop caring, and the whole enterprise may eventually drift apart.

6.5. And If They're Still Not Buying It?

Where leadership is not entirely convinced, it's a hard fight to implement a CDL intervention. The lack of support and the lack of work that's being done at the leadership level inhibits and constrains what can be done at lower levels. So even if a CDL practitioner has been approached by the HR department, or some other role-player in the organisation, it may not be a good idea to work with an organisation that is not completely convinced of the importance of CDL in the first place.

Leaders who have not properly bought into the process will

1. Try to dictate the terms of the intervention

2. Encourage you to steer away from certain 'difficult' topics and focus on others

3. See CDL as a way to *manage the problems of difference away* rather than *creatively engage with human diversity*

4. Unreasonably limit the exposure of staff members to CDL precepts

Ultimately, whether or not you opt to work with organisations that have not fully bought into CDL is up to you. Here are some of the pros and cons of working with problematic companies.

6.5.1.   Arguments *Against* Working with Problematic Companies

Critical approaches to diversity are theoretically and philosophically rich endeavours and allowing them to be framed in ways that clash with their core beliefs can compromise the commitments and the integrity of practitioners.

For people in oppressed positionalities within an organisation, a CDL intervention can be a sign of hope. If leadership does not support it, then at the end of the day there will be no change because there is no hope, and the practitioner will have become complicit in a betrayal of people within the organisation.

Very often, our processes mean that people will walk out of workshops where the brunt of the discomfort, or the painful work of facing up to oppressive systems, will have been done by those most marginalized in those organisations. To ask people to do this work without leadership buy-in is also potentially to betray their trust.

> *It's an unacceptable trade-off to do "comfortable" work. ... You sacrifice your integrity and the integrity of the process.... This work should be about inviting people into discomfort....*

> **– Melanie Judge**

Often, organisations that call in CDL facilitators are doing so only because of pressure they are facing from an external source and are not honestly committing to any kind of internal change.

> *They just want us to come in, and then they want to prescribe to us how we must do it, or what we're allowed to do.... And those kinds of situations can backfire, because obviously what needs to happen is something much deeper and more thorough than what they're willing to agree to or what they're comfortable with. And that can become a disaster, because it opens up all this stuff and then there's no other room for real engagement.*

> **– Haley McEwen**

People in organisations may remember older, failed diversity interventions that prevent them from wanting to engage with future ones. Asking marginalised people to do the emotional work involved in a CDL intervention with no clear sense that it will be leading anywhere jeopardises not only the process itself, but future processes too. Staff have sat through workshops like yours before, and not heard what the outcome is, and never had any feedback from leadership. After such disillusionment, why would they sign up for the second or third workshop, to be retraumatised by a different facilitator?

There is a performative dimension to discussions about human diversity, a performance of remorse and guilt or performances of pain that expose wounds. If this is being done for no real purpose, or merely to soothe the consciences of the powerful groups that sustain the oppressive systems, the intervention must be avoided at all costs.

6.5.2.   Arguments *for* Working with Problematic Companies

> *Oppression has a psychological impact on people, especially Black people, that is essentially the same as gaslighting. The oppressor makes you think that you are crazy for feeling the way you do. So I believe it's really important that people learn the language to realise no, it's not me, I'm not the crazy one.*

– Busi Dlamini

Sometimes, even the most problematic companies have people inside them that will gain a lot from a CDL intervention and could even spark positive change. Just having access to a language to talk about privilege and oppression even if leadership is not fully on board can be a transformative experience for team members.

People within the organisation do not always have the opportunity to leave. They are held ransom by worry that without this job, they will have no income. Having access to the language of CDL might be an important liberatory experience for these people even in contexts where leadership is not yet listening. They can't yet walk away, they don't yet have other choices, and for now they have to stay where they are. CDL can help them to interpret the world they are in, to know that they are not crazy, to help them analyse it.

Managers are generally hostile to CDL because they see that there is something subversive about the nature of what we're doing, where they can see that we are advocates for social justice and not just service providers for staff development. People's mothers and fathers and brothers and sisters are employed in these organisations, being treated in a damaging way. Do we wait for the entire system to collapse while they're feeling pain every single day? Or do we ensure that they are treated like a human being, at least for today?

Sometimes, the groups that are most disempowered by their leadership can have the most effective breakthroughs in action planning and the follow up sessions. A benefit of quite constrained working environments we have noticed in the past is that management make attendance at workshops compulsory: there is a sense that even if you aren't really onboard, you have to come to the workshop. And this can be a great advantage to the process. We can use the pressure cooker environment of some of these organisations to seed important concepts about diversity, and have positive ripple effects into the broader society, even if the organisation itself is not going to change any time soon. That alone makes the difficult clients worth working with.

6.6. Conclusion

In this chapter we have offered a variety of narratives, logics, and reasons that may be of use when contracting a CDL intervention with an organisation. The irony of this work is that it is a product that organisations want to buy and many diversity practitioners do it as their only livelihood and yet it works best when organisations leave it to the facilitator to determine what exactly goes into the package. If CDL practitioners are too eager to sell their services, and to meet the demands of management, they become ineffective as practitioners. In recent South African history, we have seen two large financial audit firm and a global management consultant enter into tailspins as the extent of the improper collusion with their clients has been revealed. There is a parallel to CDL work, which is undermined if it is captured by narrow management interests that clash with the core precepts of our model. It is of crucial importance that CDL maintains a healthy distance from the core purpose of the organisations that we work with, sticking to the important work of building capacities that can support people and organisations to challenge oppressive structures wherever they find them.

Chapter 7

How Does Change Happen?

This chapter outlines a particular "theory of change" that addresses the symptomatic picture of the organisation that cannot deal with difference we sketched in Chapter 2. Essential to our model is the idea that CDL is a *reading practice*. The design of our intervention is such that we build the diversity literacy, and thus the critical capacity of the people within the organisation, to make the changes that are required to their own organisation, themselves. Diversity practitioners cannot be parachuted into an organisation to 'fix' it: that is the work of the people who are already there, who understand their business model, who know the people, who are familiar with the specific dynamics that the organisation must contend with.

Furthermore, it is really hard to know which aspects of the problem one ought to put down to 'diversity' issues: after all, where does dealing with difference begin, and other problems of leadership, management, and external factors end? This is a frequent observation of practitioners:

> *Sometimes diversity becomes a productivity issue, or affects employee satisfaction, but it's tricky: it's hard to pin it on one particular issue. It's not just diversity, it's management style, or just the whole culture of the organisation that's a problem.*

> **– Jennie Tsekwa**

We need to ask ourselves why organisations struggle so much to deal with difference: i.e., why the fact of *difference* introduces *discord* into the organisation instead of *engagement*. CDL has a particular theoretical approach to this question that we will outline below. Then we need to ask ourselves what the end state is, i.e., what are the signs that an organisation is dealing with difference not as discord, but as an opportunity for engagement? Finally, we will look at what critical success factors need to be in place for this transformation to happen.

7.1. Difference as Discord

In this section we paint a causal picture of the discordant organisation: i.e., why does it manifest the kind of malaise that we described in Chapter 1? From our experience working with organisations, seen through the appropriate theoretical frameworks, we have distilled the following list of the root causes of difference as discord within organisations.

7.1.1.   'Closed' Cultural Systems

Very often an organisation's orientation around its internal culture and the relationship of that culture to the society it exists in determines how it deals with difference. Discordant organisations typically aspire to be *closed cultural systems* that can stop the problems of the world at their doors. Often, these organisations will pride themselves on a unique internal culture that they try to protect from 'contamination' by the problems of the outside world. They will thus often address racial, sexual, or gender difference with a kind of wishful thinking about values: they will claim to be "colour-blind" or to celebrate "sheroes" during Women's Month. These organisations grapple with social problems by reinterpreting them as wolves that can be kept from the door. This kind of messaging may play a particular role in the institutional environment, but the home environment, and the nature of economic circumstances outside of the organisation, remind people that the world is neither equal nor equitable: critical reflection back on the organisation reminds them that gestures towards unattainable ideals are part and parcel of reproducing inequality.

In these organisations, staff are encouraged to leave parts of themselves at home: to split themselves between a work persona, and a home persona. They may even be rewarded for not allowing home life to affect work life:

- For not letting their roles as parents reduce the availability of their energy and their time for tasks in the organisational context.

- For not being offended, or just taking it as a joke, when a colleague makes discriminatory remarks about the group to which they belong.

- For not contextualising issues within the work environment within their appropriate political, social, or economic histories, for example in opposing or hindering the formation of workers' unions.

The idea that the world outside the office is full of contradiction, discord, and politics, but that the boundaries of the institution offer a temporary respite from these stormy seas is of course an encoded way of enforcing a particular politics, a particular way of seeing the world, which is typically that of the leadership structure (and laden with protection of its various privileges). Think for example of the language of 'professionalism'. Many organisations value the 'professionalism' of their staff, when it is clear that:

- Men access professionalism through societally entrenched norms that construct them as rational (i.e., less emotional) and competitive.

- White people (in the South African as in so many other contexts) capitalise on centuries of the social construction of the 'competence' supposedly arising from their 'innate' abilities and cultures.

- Access to particular educational environments is highly classed at every level of schooling and further education which creates shared norms and scripts of competence shared by the groups that have had access to these institutions.

Members of 'closed system' organisations are thus urged to reproduce these discriminatory cultures, which masquerade as 'professional' or 'competitive' or just 'the way we do things here', for reasons that may ultimately serve a particular power structure. Often, these cultures reproduce themselves most acutely in intensive mentorship relationships that focus on people from specific groups, or even reproduce historical cultures through seemingly 'diverse' bodies. The fact is that many organisational cultures exist in order to distract attention from societal contradictions. A private school must pride itself on its 'excellence' and that of its students in order to distract attention from the fact that its performance is almost entirely reducible to the average socioeconomic status of its learners and the fact that it has thousands of times the budget of a rural public school. Norms of corporate leave-taking for child-rearing which 'favour' women reproduce the idea that it is normal for the bulk of this work to fall on women in the first place. The people within the institutions around whose bodies the institution has formed are thus comforted by its culture. They are led to believe that their preferences, the things that make them feel happy and valued, are in fact an objectively verifiable principle of 'professionalism' or 'excellence'. This creates an organisational context where, for example, you've got predominantly white males who then hire white females and they form a 'club' of professionals, who actually define what they do not on the basis of biography but on the basis of their 'competence'. So the organisational vision and the skills mix becomes the focal point, and people become completely insensitive to the fact that they all look the same.

The comfort of the people that these cultures serve is thereby constructed as the only guarantor of the organisation's ultimate aim of its profitability, or sustainability, or its academic standards. The idea of organisations as insular entities, where we are all united to drive results, constructs people who challenge that unity as trouble-causers, people who rock the boat and thus threaten the ultimate aim. The disciplinary power of the organisation is very often in winning over otherwise critical minds into an acceptance of organisational culture as the only way to do this. Paradoxically, then, the closed organisation understands how fragile it is, as very often the model is based on the fragility of profit or excellence. This fragility offers cover for an extreme sensitivity around change, around challenge to established norms, and is indicative of the protection of established narrow interests.

7.1.2.   Powerful Resistors: Internalised Dominance

People in power tend to be the arbiters of the internal culture, and they enact that on a day-to-day basis, subtly or not so subtly undermining actions that are being taken to change it. It is not impossible that these people should be part of positive change in the organisation in fact, they are absolutely crucial for it but very often they do not appreciate the full extent to which they have internalised their own dominant positionalities. They are very often rendered incapable of any critical analysis of their own positions. Why should this be so?

The short answer is that they become heavily invested in *not* questioning their own right to have the power and the positions they hold:

> *For example, men are heavily invested in the dividends of patriarchal power. They reap material rewards, symbolic rewards, and investing in the protection of their right to these rewards is quite clearly related to their identity, quite literally to who they are in the world. As a white person, as a straight person, your investments are so heavy and so deep and they have such long histories, it becomes hard to say, 'No, I want to destabilise this, I want to disrupt and untangle it'.*

–Melanie Judge

Many of the people running organisations today are operating in environments they have always been familiar with, with the kinds of people they have known all their lives, and with social contexts in which they feel completely comfortable. They participate in very homogenous social circles, and yet are, more often than not, unaware of just how homogeneous these circles are. White South Africans, for example, mostly grow up in majority white suburbs, go to majority white schools, spaces that were formed by apartheid. People are not sufficiently encouraged to take the time to reflect critically on that with which they are familiar and make a commitment to change it. They are simply happy to perpetuate the status quo. Even if at some point they may become motivated to be critical of their upbringing and privileges, their own interests and those of their families, and friends, are so powerful that they form an anchor mooring them in a particular way of viewing social life.

This does not mean that people in dominant subject positions are not moved by injustice, inequality, or the urgency of change. It does however often mean that instead of engaging with these facts at a structural level and critiquing their own complicity and the ways in which they benefit, they will adopt a 'rescue mentality' that merely reproduces their dominance. Much corporate voluntarism and charity fall into this category: they dissipate the social justice energy of individuals in projects that coddle the self-image of privileged people, and therefore are unable to challenge existing power arrangements in any meaningful way. These dysfunctional orientations are common in certain liberal discourses, and both reproduce and centralise the good white person / good man / good rich person. True allyship is more demanding, as it undermines that assumption that the powerful get to decide the nature of a particular project, and avoids the idea of a rescue in favour of a position of solidarity in realigning power relations.

7.1.3. Powerful Resistors: Internalised Oppression

Processes of racial, class, or gender identification are not sufficient to determine one's consciousness of social location: Some people fully buy into this system. Often, this is because they have managed to 'play the game' in a way for which they deserve recognition and are unwilling to see the ways in which they were themselves useful as exceptions rather than the proving of a new rule. They actually become foot soldiers for reproducing the management paradigm: our female/disabled/Black bodies are here for their excellence, we are here because our skills drive the organisation's success, and we don't want to been seen as anything else other than that.

This can be completely sincere of course; it can also be a conscious bargain in problematic environments, where assimilation becomes a way to cope with structural problems, to avoid falling foul of the local power structures. They tend to feel a sense of achievement: I've made it into this white world and look at me, I'm the only Black person here. This links into an aspirational psychology: You want to be with the dominant group, you want to be like them, because they're the embodiment of competence. This makes it exceptionally difficult for people who are losing out to speak up in any meaningful way. If they do, they are often constructed as the 'trouble causers'.

The consequence of this institutional assimilation is the oft-documented phenomenon of the reproduction of organisational policies and cultures that harm certain groups being reproduced by people from those very groups. Institutional cultures can survive in insidious ways, especially in defence of ideals such as 'profit' or 'excellence,' or in the case of tertiary education, 'internationally recognised'.

What this means is that, while the actual composition of the board and the top levels of management of an organisation is an important indicator of how much an organisation has transformed, it is not on its own a sufficient indicator. A Black CEO does not eradicate racism; a person with a disability in a senior position does not automatically make the workplace friendly to disabled people. Especially in the cases of pioneers and mavericks, who have always been exceptions in their field, they may have psychologically held themselves ransom to the very power structures that they were fighting to overcome in the first place.

Another dimension to internalised dominance is of course that members of powerful groups might exploit these psychological states to shore up their own power. They will knowingly appoint members of underrepresented groups to senior positions in order to defuse the dissatisfaction of staff more broadly. The only way to find out the extent to which difference is discordant in an organisation is to actually ask the people working there.

7.1.4. Focus on Intentions

The mantra of the discordant organisation is that discrimination only happens when it can be proven that it was *intended*. The focus on intentions is based on a naïve theory of disadvantage: that the problem starts and ends with the way people treat each other, and that it is only morally wrong to treat a person badly if you are aware that your treatment of them is motivated by their race/sex/gender/sexuality/ability/etc.

There are a number of different reasons why this naïve theory of disadvantage doesn't hold up, linked into the 10 principles of CDL. Some of the key challenges to put to people who hold the naïve view include:

- The real sources of disadvantage and discrimination in the workplace tend to be generally accepted cultural principles, company policies, or standard operating procedures that reproduce assumptions about who they think belongs here, how they should behave, and why. These general rules do not rely on an individual intention to discriminate: they are codified, normalised, and often unquestioned. Trying to track down the intentions of the original framers of the policies, or influencers of the organisational culture, is a wild goose chase: a waste of time and energy that would have been better spent changing the policies, assumptions, and culture of the organisation. The status quo might not be *'intended'* but positive change relies very much on our intending to do it and seeing that change through.

- The workings of power are often not visible to powerful people. People in powerful social locations, whether they realise it or not, tend to take their own structural advantages for granted, and can easily universalize their own experience of the world to other people. It can be hard for able-bodied people to understand why a disabled person can't "take a joke" when they themselves have had to "take a joke" in some other dimension of their lives. It is clear that these "jokes" can be harmful, and that this harm need not be intended. Much harm is initiated from a state of ignorance, or unconscious bias, not from conscious intention.

- Because most of us claim a commitment to free and equal treatment and have repeated the usual pieties about how racism is wrong, and sexism is wrong, etc., it can be hard to admit that we are morally implicated in discriminatory social formations. There is thus a strong incentive for us to deny our own involvement, and to preserve our own sense of innocence. An organisation is not a court of law, and a transformation process is not a trial. The burden of proof is very different. This is the basic reason why our own reporting of intentions is not relevant to establishing whether an organisational environment is discriminatory or not. A far more reliable indicator is listening to the experiences of people who report the negative effects they feel, tapping into the experiences and anger of the 'trouble-causers' as much as possible, and focusing on remedial action at both a structural and cultural level.

- Some people do hold racist/sexist/ableist/etc. views and some people sometimes intend to do social damage to others through withholding opportunity, through verbal abuse, or some other form of harassment. But even in these cases, where intention becomes more salient, proving that a particular insult/action was directly motivated by a desire to discriminate based on race/sex/ability/etc., while relevant to disciplinary action, is a red herring at the level of organisational improvement. Creating an engaging environment for difference is a completely different process to disciplinary action and cannot be held hostage to the same rules.

7.1.5. Reading Social Constructions as Immutable Realities

Another naïve view of discrimination is that the racist bigot or male chauvinist holds an entirely negative view of the racial/sexual Other. On the contrary: group-based discrimination often subsists in the assertion of supposedly positive qualities:

- Women are maternal, loving, caring, sensitive, considerate.

- Black people are friendly, hardworking, uncomplaining, religious.

- Homosexuals are fashionable, creative, fun to have around.

- Indian people are good with money, family-oriented, and modest.

Frequently it's the cis-gendered heterosexual white males whose qualities are held up as those best suited to senior leadership roles:

- White men are decisive, visionary, know when to take risks, uncompromising, level-headed, rational, professional, self-correcting, honest.

Of course negative qualities are an important part of these cartoonish portraits, but more often than not the negative quality slides under the assertion of the positive: women's emotional intelligence is constructed in opposition to 'real' intelligence, or the cool-headed rationality considered necessary to steering a company; Black people's supposed 'friendliness' is asserted as a cover for an implied simplicity and corruptibility; homosexuals are 'fun' and therefore need not be taken too seriously. When members of groups exhibit unexpected qualities 'cold' women, Black people who complain they are vilified as being unnatural, as being problematic exceptions that let the whole side down.

7.2.   Difference as Engagement

The desired end-state organisation is largely a creature of the imagination: for the most part, the place we describe here does not yet exist. However, it is useful to think through just what kind of environment we are hoping to move towards.

Organisational approaches to workforce diversity can be represented as a continuum[88], arranged from least to most desirable. On one end of the continuum, we find an orientation that denies there is anything to transform, while at the opposite end of the continuum, there is an orientation in which diversity is embedded in all dimensions of organisational life; actively fostered not only inside the organisation, but also throughout its external relationships.

Frame 1: It's Fixed. Don't break it

The most difficult and intractable way of framing a discussion about transformation is having to argue about whether it is necessary or not. There are people who doggedly hold the position that transformation has already happened, that no racism or other forms of oppression exist in their departments or teams or organisations, that "colour doesn't matter anymore", and so forth. Here transformation is framed as an unwanted form of social engineering that is geared to raise unnatural expectations and disturb the supposedly peaceful status quo.

---

[88] These approaches were adapted to the South African context by Rejane Williams, from the discussion in "The Future of Workplace Diversity in the New Millennium" by the diversity consultants Tony Montes and Graham Shaw (2003).

Frame 2: Compliance

Sometimes transformation is framed as a matter of complying with equity-related policies and targets, for example those set by government or by an institution's board or executive management. It is essentially a technocratic approach in which transformation is reduced to following certain procedures and ticking prescribed boxes. This orientation is rarely driven by a heartfelt commitment to change, but rather relies on efficient systems for avoiding penalties. If external pressure were to be removed, transformation would not be a priority.

Frame 3: Wanting to Help

This orientation moves beyond legal compliance and places emphasis on helping disadvantaged groups the kind of dysfunctional rescuing that we will discuss below in §8.1.4. Transformation is mostly framed as a one-way process, with the generous and fortunate reaching out to welcome or assist those in need. The inherent paternalism of this approach is often unconscious, with the dominant actors having no sense of their own need to transform. In an organisational context, it may also manifest in superficial celebrations of diversity, conducted in ways that overlook issues of power and inequality.

Frame 4: Diversity is an Asset

A fourth way that transformation is sometimes framed is to see diversity as a competitive advantage, as a process of gathering or catalysing diverse skills and experiences, and as a prerequisite for innovation and dynamic development. In business organisations, this means actively pursuing a diverse work force because it is believed to make "business sense". This frame typically also allows more types of diversity to be brought into the spotlight, and attention may be paid to removing barriers to participation and creating opportunities that redress historic imbalances.

Frame 5: A Transformative Purpose

Adopting this frame for understanding transformation means making it a core value and strategy. It acknowledges multiple diversities, as well as the complex and dynamic nature of change. In this orientation, transformation is seen as an ongoing process, which will always be part of society, and therefore has no final completion date. In organisations, the aim is to integrate transformation into all other organisational functions and strategies. It is not a separate project, but rather lives and breathes through the whole organisation. This perspective may even look beyond the boundaries of an organisation or institution itself. Here transformation is framed as an organisational, community-wide, national and even global imperative. It is fully integrated into organisational practice and recognises the complex and permeable boundaries between organisations and the larger economy, public sector and civil society. Transformation is part of building strong organisations, just as it is part of building a strong economy, a strong population and a strong society.

We will briefly discuss some of the things that we believe one would observe at this fifth level, where difference is seen as an opportunity to engage, and not the seed of discord.

7.2.1. Dynamic Cultural Systems

Here the organisation is understood as continuous with society and in a dynamic and interdependent relationship with it, where societal and community health are indistinguishable from organisational health. These organisations do not wait for the world to change, nor do they pretend that the charity or volunteer action spurred by an internal marketing campaign is anything more than leveraging a good cause to attract kudos from staff and specific stakeholders. Open, dynamic organisations understand that they are structurally implicated in the world, and work to address the very rules of engagement.

These organisations are willing to position themselves at the leading edge: their policies on parental leave will envision radical gender and sexual equality; their demographics will represent the demographics of the country; they will concern themselves with long-term engagement with the political and social currents.

7.2.2. People as Free and Equal

When difference is being engaged productively, the philosophical space to discuss freedom and equality is opened up. Within the organisation, difference is constantly being spoken about in such a way that it not a lapse into inequality. Access to power and voice are carefully managed, and the model of the organisation thrives on the innovations that come from people solving problems that directly affect their lives in an organic and immediate way, rather than being driven from the top down.

7.2.3. People as Works in Progress

The organisation engaging with difference does not expect its members to be finished products, and never to step on each other's toes. People are works in progress. They come to the organisational environment with attachments to histories of privilege and oppression, and the conversational space therefore needs to be kept open for them to engage in these histories and realities.

7.2.4. Focus on Experiences

The organisation that sees difference as an opportunity for engagement takes seriously people's reports of their own experiences of discrimination and inequality within the organisation and does not approach these questions with a legalistic focus on intentions. Leadership structures organise themselves to assess the structural basis for people's experience of discord and open up space for people to engage in transformative conversations with people about what happened, without (depending on the seriousness of the offence) first jumping into the space of discipline and punishment.

People are believed when they speak up, because the history of silencing of groups who have been on the receiving end of discrimination, oppression, and abuse is recognised and actively counteracted in internal culture and the assumptions about what did and did not happen.

7.2.5. Attention to the Histories and Futures of Social Constructions

All of these aspects of the organisation successfully dealing with difference are grounded in close attention to the ways that team members are bound to interact with powerful social constructions that are both historical (and structural) legacies and pose potential future problems, especially if they are not dealt with in the present. If harmful social divisions are not to forever haunt the organisation, then they need to be consciously exorcised from the premises in the present.

7.3. Critical Success Factors

If the organisation is to make the transition, then whatever capacity-building intervention is done would be greatly aided by particular success factors. This does not mean that we absolutely cannot do the work if these are not in place merely that these are good conditions with which to work.

7.3.1. Leadership Buy-In

> *Where leadership at the most senior level is committed to fairness, and believe in changing things at a personal, interpersonal, institutional and systemic level I think that no matter how much resistance is in that system, I think one can make it work.*

> – **Kirsten Klopper**

Leadership is not just expected to say: "we believe in it, now go and do the work". They need to be visible in in the process, to participate in the sessions, to show their presence and their engagement. Their active advocacy and championing of the work within the organisation is required to ensure that it has a chance of success. Leadership will be grappling with their own issues, but if they show a genuine willingness to go through the process with their team, then there is a much better chance of success. The reverse is also true: many practitioners comment that if the CEO (or headmaster, or vice-chancellor) is not actively engaged in the process, you are wasting your time.

> *People complain: where is the management, they need to be in this workshop. I think that it's felt very deeply. Sometimes transformation work is seen as the work of Black people, usually by the white management team. Many organisations have mostly Black staff on their transformation committees, and white people have the attitude of "oh well, you people have this issue, so you go and fix it".*

> **– Pierre Brouard**

Leaders who do their own work—who are willing to read up on diversity issues and to engage in their own personal development journeys—are especially useful. It gives practitioners the license to do some of the more challenging work within the organisation.

When CDL is only built as a capacity within the human resources team, some of this challenging work tends to become more difficult. The opportunity of having an external provider come in board can result in bolder, more risk-taking interventions. Indeed, transformation as a whole requires courage from leaders.

> *One senior leader I have worked with knows he needs to hire more Black staff. But he is worried about how it will be perceived by the existing team. And I just wanna tell him: just do it! Pull yourself together, don't worry about what other people think, if it's the right thing to do it's the right thing to do, you're the leader! You know. It's funny how even leaders who have loads of business experience or long histories of making tough decisions suddenly when it comes to diversity start tiptoeing around it....*

> **– Jennie Tsekwa**

7.3.2. Thoroughgoing Momentum

Institutions that think of a diversity intervention as a once-off event, a Band-Aid to put onto some difference-related scratches, are bound to not see the process through, and might end up doing more harm to their teams than good. A critical success factor is that the organisation understands at its highest levels that its very core needs to shift, in order to become a healthier, more engaged, and more effective institutions.

> *You always need to have an eye on how your intervention fits into the bigger transformation agenda. If it is not thoroughgoing, so much gets lost. So it's like: we go to a workshop, and now what? There is a specific case of this, where we go through the first phase, which was quite disruptive but also quite powerful. And then it was two years later before anybody heard anything. So even though leadership was on board, the momentum got lost, and people became quite despairing. We were all excited about doing this work, and then nothing happened.*

– Kirsten Klopper

When the goodwill of the team is squandered, and the momentum is lost, it is very easy for the relationship with the over-arching project to sour to the extent that people who otherwise would have been supportive become hostile. Keeping momentum can of course be very challenging. There are no shortcuts to building relationships; it takes time. Company policies need to be reviewed. Cultural assumptions need to be shifted in a number of practices and procedures. Both daily commitment and long-term vision are required.

> *Leadership must take a long view. This change is slow, it is incremental, it's organic, it needs to be built as small fires that smoulder here and there. And eventually it needs to be backed up by good policies.*

– Pierre Brouard

Without momentum through the long haul, the organisation remains mired in a reactive mode, unable to proactively open up spaces for dealing with issues before they even arise. Organisations should think very carefully about their ability to see the process through before they embark. The negative consequences of a half-hearted or incomplete process can exacerbate existing tensions; they can also sap energy and commitment in advance from any future diversity interventions.

> *I've seen some other organisations get halfway into their transformation project and then stop it because of budget constraints or whatever. And that is the worst ever! Because then it totally convinces everyone, 'yup, we knew this from the start, this wasn't for real, we should never even have started'.*

Then five years down the line when a new diversity intervention is launched, because there has of course been another crisis, so much energy is lost in just convincing people that this thing won't merely repeat all of their negative experiences!

– Jennie Tsekwa

7.3.3.   Internal Communication

While leadership must be sincerely involved, they must also be seen to be sincerely involved: the buy-in of leadership and the rationale for the process must be marketed and communicated within the organisation, even as the details of the project and its impacts are communicated. Both the 'what' and the 'how' of the communication are very important.

Important 'what' questions include: who is involved, what will they do, and is it mandatory or voluntary? The 'what' must of course also include a 'then what?'. What are the outcomes? How will this be cascaded? How much time are we going to devote to it? Where does it stand in relation to our other priorities? In terms of the 'how': are staff being ordered to support the process, or are they being invited? Is it seen as an exciting opportunity, or imbued with the heavy weight of compliance and the technical language of missed transformation targets?

Because much of the communication gets done before CDL has been built as a capacity in the organisation, the message about what it actually is can easily get distorted. At the same time, identifying an internal 'expert' department comes with its own pitfalls. While many organisations will choose to delegate the entire process to the HR department, care should be taken to ensure that teams and their leaders within the organisations are taking the process seriously and communicating it as a core and critical change process.

The leadership who really get it should be the ones to communicate it. This might include HR, as long as they really get it. They should focus on communicating: this is our vision, this is what we're wanting to do, this is why we're wanting to do it, this is what it's gonna look like, these are the kinds of sacrifices we will ask you to make in terms of time, this is the picture of where it fits in the whole organisational transformation strategy. If they don't answer those questions, and they aren't prepared to be very visible and present in that process, and it's not just you as an external consultant coming in, then the very people who've been asking for the change will feel very suspicious and actually not come to the table.

– Jennie Tsekwa

Team members often express not wanting to be excluded from the planning process, especially if they are directly affected by low levels of CDL in the organisation. The change process cannot simply be imposed on them. They will question whether the organisational leadership are doing this for the right reasons, are whether they are just doing this to pacify their unruly staff. This is especially relevant in environments where there is not a great deal of trust in leadership, who might be directly implicated in the reproduction of discordant organisational habits.

7.3.4. Time and Resources

In order truly to sustain the momentum of a thoroughgoing and deep process, adequate time and resources have to be devoted to it. Staff will read the level of commitment of their leadership in terms of the kinds of resources they are willing to devote to something not necessarily large budgets, but large amounts of attention, care, and emphasis. If people need to take time away from their day-to-day tasks to be part of a process, who will fill their role while they are away? Or will they be expected to sit in workshops with their phones on, disrupting the process and checking out every time there is something they need to attend to? Management chooses to attach specific meanings to activities and processes through the way they show what they value. If a workshop is just ticking a box, and the actual time and attention of participants is not secured, it is bound to fail.

Successful change processes do not obscure the fact that they are actually quite time-consuming. Doing things differently might, initially at least, actually increase the workload of team members.

> *One unit I have worked with has put so much effort into the shifts that are required. They now support developmental initiatives that are not necessarily at the core of their function, in order to ensure that their aspiration to equity is actually lived. They have this added commitment that it's not just about your job description. They understand that workshops are not the work, that they're only supporting the change. They have this ability to try new ideas out, and to fail, and to have courage to course-correct. I think sometimes they're too hard on themselves, and I worry that they will end up burned out.*

– Busi Dlamini

The work of building CDL is not linear, and the process we design as practitioners is only one factor that influences it. Most team members in organisations will have their own sense of social justice, no matter how deep or shallow, and many will be doing their own work in their own time. Many will take the work of transforming their organisations seriously, and personally, once it becomes clear that their input is welcomed and supported. The time and resources needed to transform an organisation are already inside it, waiting to be unlocked.

7.3.5.   Internal Agency

That the *potential* already lies in the organisation is one thing to observe; to keep the process on course and to maintain momentum does however require high level process management and a commitment to making the process work. The calibre of the person that drives transformation within the organisation (if they have such a position) is crucial. In our work we've often been shocked at how problematic transformation managers are. They perpetuate specific problems; often, they have very selective politics. They will devote all of their attention to racial redress, while reproducing patriarchal, ableist, or homophobic structures within the example, for example. This kind of transformation management is especially common in organisations that have side-lined the function, pushing it to the margins of the organisation where the voices of all of the team members are unable to influence it.

The point is to unlock the internal agency of the organisation: so while having a person responsible for transformation may be a good sign of commitment, they should see their role increasingly as a way to include more of the perspectives of marginalised people within the organisation, and to unlock the agency of all within it to be agents of positive change. It should go without saying that the same is true of external diversity practitioners who are contracted in. Their job is not to solve problems for people, but to support people in their own problem-solving, in the paradigm case presented by this manual, through building CDL.

Incumbent on facilitators to remember that the point is to build internal capacity, to work with the agency in the room

> *The best drivers of critical diversity work are actually communities and organisations and individuals who in some form come from a place of a connection with the margin. That's your most powerful thing. So whether it's queers, whether it's Black feminists... so those are really the ones who will bring real political will, for certain kinds of interventions.*

– Melanie Judge

Often, engagement with the CDL process will only be one part of the whole story of personal development that these drivers of critical diversity are engaging in. They do their own work:

Whether it's reading on their own, or taking time to reflect... And there's something deeper than just doing research. It's also realising that are not exposed enough to difference in your own life, and going out there to get exposed and to open yourself up to other people.

— **Jennie Tsekwa**

7.3.6. Working with Stakeholders

In larger organisations, or ones that are intimately interconnected with stakeholder groups, it might not be enough to work only with the people who are 'inside' the institution. Customers and suppliers to large corporations, organisational Boards, unions, donors to the NGO sector, the students representative council members and broader political structures of universities, alumni, parents at schools, and so on, all form part of the immediate relevant environment of the organisation and impact on its ability to change, as well as impacted on by any changes that happen.

The idea of working in closed-off, monolithic, homogenous organisations or communities is simply impossible. You can't actually operate in isolation anymore; you can't get away with it. But that does create certain possibilities I think also. One example is the LGBT sector. The sector had become racially siloed some organisations that were largely working with white constituencies and then there were organisations that are largely working with Black constituencies diversity they could only become receptive to issues at the intersection of race and sexuality once they understood themselves and their stakeholders holistically.

— **Melanie Judge**

Parents and schools can be critical anchors on any change process within schools, undoing important work on the one hand, or on the other hand not being included to a level that would make them positive agents for change. The answers to some of an organisation's most pressing challenges are very often already being articulated by somebody in its stakeholder group; working with that group can be the push they need.

7.3.7. Risk-Taking

The organisation's appetite for doing things differently plays a big role in whether or not they will be able to move towards higher diversity literacy... If they are convinced that the way they are doing things right now is the best way until they can find another that has absolute certainty attached to it, there is little hope that they will be able to take the plunge into fully engaging with difference in society.

You can have leaders who say, 'we wanna be diverse, we wanna be diverse'. Are they really ready for it, or do they even grasp what it means to share power with people that they are not that familiar with? There's a deep comfort issue. So you can even have a diverse leadership team, but who really holds the power? Who does the CEO really trust to get things done?

– Jennie Tsekwa

Often, consultants will feel under pressure to provide positive feedback to the leadership team, to underplay the risks, in order to prevent fear from ending their contract. Instead of providing an accurate mirror to the organisation, they try to flatter it. The balance is to make it clear that while the work really needs to be done, and that there will be big risks along the way to getting it done, the biggest risk of all is in hoping the problem will go away on its own. Sometimes as we have seen in recent months with some prominent South African brands and people the risk has the power to actually end the organisation as people know it.

At the same time, even small and tentative steps towards improving the organisation's ability to deal with difference indicate that there is hope that things will change. It is easy to become judgmental, to blame organisations for being stuck at a particular level in their development. Oftentimes it is risk aversion that keeps them stuck; as a diversity practitioner you can be of assistance by appropriately measuring and managing the risks that they face and helping to put them in some perspective.

7.3.8. Measuring Progress

Transformation is ideally on the Board agenda and is part of what is measured from Board meeting to Board meeting. In corporate settings, close and intentional management of transformation indicators might include their being tied to financial incentives. People tend to exhibit the behaviours and deliver the results that they know they are going to be rewarded for. These rewards can of course be affirmative, or link in to their own sense of personal development. But if a company rewards certain outputs higher sales, a successful marketing campaign with material incentives, and treats meeting transformation goals as a poor second cousin to real results, this sends the wrong signal to the team.

Of course, transformation should be "heart-work" and in most settings that will be the most sustainable and powerful way to frame it. But if it is to be included in the organisation's definition of success, then it is important to track and reward progress against the plan as assiduously and carefully as any other indicator. Ultimately, though the required change is cultural, we cannot afford to be dismissive of the numbers, to discount the quantitative dimensions of transformation. Though the measurable indicators of transformation should not be the driving motivation for change as we have pointed out in problematising compliance they do have to play a role. There is no escaping this.

The staff of the organisation the teams you are trying to work with will often insist on knowing what the numbers are. It helps to have a visible scorecard that can be referred to, and accessible to staff throughout the process. Doing this empowers people to participate in tracking their own progress, and in locating their everyday work towards a more inclusive organisation against an organisational plan at a very practical level. Showing where the organisation is falling short of course also makes transparent to the team what the problems are and engages a broader team of people in problem-solving. This is clearly not risk-free: people might feel singled out or stigmatised on the basis of belonging to a powerful group. This kind of communication thus needs to be done with humanity and sensitivity. Transformation so often consists mostly of rhetoric; the challenge is in the doing, and grappling and wrestling with 'what does equity look like' at its most fundamental practical, and measurable level.

One of the many up-sides of close and careful measurements is that they provide the opportunity for the team to celebrate progress against targets. These kinds of celebrations are absolutely crucial for building and sustaining momentum in a change process. The let the whole team know that for all of the discomfort, and for the risks they are taking, real rewards are starting to accrue.

7.4.   Summary and Conclusion

We covered five aspects of the discordant organisation, and then imagined very briefly what these five aspects look like in organisations that manage to engage productively with difference. We then considered eight critical success factors for implementing CDL work in organisations to move them from discordant, to engaged. In the next two chapters, we are going to get more specific about process design: how to ensure you get the most out of the intervention.

What we now need to discuss is the size of the task that we actually take on in working against the directionality of power, in order to try to change ossified and 'time-honoured' ways of dealing with difference which oppress and harm people within organisations. In the next chapter, we focus on working "against the flow".

Chapter 8

Working 'Against the Flow'

Building critical diversity literacy in the organisational context is bound to meet powerful and resilient pockets of resistance. These especially tenacious structures of thinking are thus the focus of this chapter. Because very often the most powerful people in an organisation are also those most resistant to change, it is easy for the opposition to overwhelm practitioners, and completely derail an important process. We need to understand that organisations are in trouble because they have a particular way of doing things, a 'flow' that most people go with and that our job is often to go 'against the flow'.

An issue that undergirds resistance is the idea that organisations should focus on an inspiring vision for the future, and not get bogged down in the past. Our approach to this past/future dichotomy is to break it down. We agree (as spelled out in Chapter 5) that "The past is not dead. It isn't even past". The past lives with us and in us in the present, in intimate interconnections with the future. There is no future that does not take the past with it. The only question is what we will do in the present to impact on those connections.

People who insist that we should "leave the past behind" and rather "focus on the future" are thus asking for something that is not really possible the past will always affect us. But they are also asking for something that is dangerous, in that if we don't examine how it affects us, we are likely to reproduce its harmful patterns. Ignoring the past is thus what really gets us stuck in it; facing up to it, confronting its legacies and entanglements, is what gives us the hope of moving on.

In this chapter we focus on how to deal with three particularly thorny areas of resistance: (1) established patterns of privilege, internalised oppression, and domination; (2) whiteness as a specific system of power; and (3) resistance to moving outside of emotional comfort zones. In the fourth section, we spend some time discussing the future, and how CDL unlocks profoundly important conversations about organisational vision, before briefly summarising the argument in the final section.

8.1. Working with: Privilege, Dominance, and Oppression

In this section, we will discuss privilege, oppression, and domination as interconnected phenomena. These are of course all power relations, and the appropriate subject of this section thus really is power and how it plays out in the organisational context.

8.1.1.   Privilege

The notion of "white/male/cis-gendered/abled/Western privilege" has become a kind of political football in recent years, and a central term of contention in the 'new' culture wars. It is worth recapping some of the key terms of this debate, even though the concept itself has become hackneyed. We will approach it in terms how to respond to the major objections.

Objection 1: "I Have Not Had an Easy Life!"

Having privilege does not imply that everything has been easy[89]. You can be the holder of various privileges and still end up in poverty, in prison, or be the victim of discrimination. The philosopher Lewis R. Gordon[90] suggests that the notion of "privilege" is something of a red herring: it conjures up images of well-healed patrons of country clubs letting valets park their cars. In fact, when we speak of "privilege" it is more like a "license" something that you have, that can give you access to certain rights and spaces, that is always there, but not necessarily a guarantee of success. You can "cash in" your privilege when you need to, and it will always give you some advantage, but it is not proof against any eventuality. People with privilege still work hard, compete with each other and with people who do not share their privilege, and might do more or less well than their peers. The point is that they have always had an advantage, an edge, over others.

So, for example, it is both true that *all* white people in South Africa share white privilege, and that *some* white people (between 1 and 2 percent) live in poverty[91]. Privilege doesn't necessarily make you feel like a special person or a particularly happy one either[92].

Objection 2: "But I Don't Feel Privileged"

People tend to compare themselves to others who are higher than themselves in the social hierarchy: white men might not feel particularly privileged when they compare themselves to Elon Musk or Bill Gates. People will deny their privilege by pointing out how stressed or unfulfilled they are as individuals. But privilege[93] often subsists in feelings of confidence in your way of looking at the world (rather than material

---

[89] This argument is unpacked in detail in Allan Johnson's book, "Privilege, power, and difference" (1997).

[90] See his article on whiteness studies, "Critical Reflections on Three Popular Tropes in the Study of Whiteness" (2004).

[91] See the AfricaCheck report on different estimates of white poverty in South Africa, which is available online (K. Wilkinson, 2016).

[92] See Johnson (1997, pp. 37–38).

[93] Our discussion here borrows a lot from the Peggy McIntosh's classic articles, "White Privilege and Male Privilege: A Personal Account of Coming to See Correspondences Through Work in Women's Studies" (1988/2011), and "White Privilege: Unpacking the Invisible Knapsack" (1989/2015).

comfort, or rock-solid self-esteem) that are proportionate to the diffidence and discomfort of others. The privileged have strong incentives *not* to see the connection between their own confidence in being right, and the power relations that enable this feeling. Not being aware of this privilege is a feature of privilege itself. Privileged people have the "luxury of obliviousness"[94] while those in less privileged positions have no choice but to be acutely aware of it, to pay close attention to the unwritten rules of the dominant culture, and to adopt "appropriate" attitudes and behaviours that dominant groups require of them. Those without privilege have to tread carefully so as not to displease those with privilege, who tend to control access to employment, resources, education and other opportunities. You might not feel your own privilege, but those around you feel it acutely, because they have had to learn to play by a set of rules that favours you.

Objection 3: "Being Privileged Means Being Exceptional"

Being privileged means being *normal*. Privilege allows people to take for granted[95] a certain level of acceptance, inclusion and respect in the world. Privilege means that you are recognised as an individual and not as a representative of a group, and that you are seen as "normal" rather than exotic, strange or anomalous. For example, media reports hardly ever refer to a "white lawyer" or "male doctor", but nearly always specify when the subject concerned is a "black pilot" or a "female engineer". Belonging to the normal group means your success is expected; belonging to some other group means your success comes as a surprise, as an exception to the rule. What this "rule" confers on the privileged is the space to assume their superiority, to make decisions, and take actions without having to worry about being challenged.

Objection 4: "If You Call Me Privileged You Are Calling Me a Bad Person"

Conservative social commentators often wrongly assume that advocates of social justice "accuse" them of privilege as if being privileged itself were a moral failing. The American scholar who is most closely associated with the development of the concept, Peggy McIntosh, reflects that "I was taught to see myself as an individual whose moral state depended on her individual moral will". This focus on an individual morality by its very definition distracts people from the power relations that structure social life, which transcend, supersede, and outlive individuals. As Allan Johnson argues,

---

[94] In the words of Johnson (1997, p. 25).
[95] See Johnson (1997, pp. 27–33).

> When it comes to privilege, then, it doesn't matter who we really are. What matters is who other people think we are, which is to say, the social categories they put us in[96].

Individuals do not *ask* for these power structures to work in their benefit, but we are responsible for *what we do* with these benefits. We can become conscious of our privilege, and work against systems that give us unfair advantage and dominance over others. The field for moral action lies is in what we *do* with our advantages and the power structures in which they are entangled and not in their existence per see.

Objection 5: "I Grew Up Privileged, But That Is Not Relevant Nowadays"

McIntosh distinguishes between *unearned advantages* and *conferred dominance*. Unearned advantages come with the way that entitlements (to things such as safety, education, health, belonging, feeling valued) are distributed in society. Nobody deserves to grow up rich or poor, it's an accident of birth: it is an unearned dis/advantage. These differences were formed in the past and are reinforced and reproduced in our everyday lives. *Conferred dominance* activates particular institutional assumptions in the here-and-now: men step into a domineering leadership style when they interrupt women; white people 'take charge' while Black people are in a deliberative dialogue; the meeting pays attention to the fluent orator, while struggling to focus on what the colleague with speech difficulties is saying. This dominance is activated in the here-and-now and builds on our unearned advantages. This provides a further case of how resilient the past is in the present.

8.1.2.   Towards a Systemic Analysis of Dominance and Oppression

People often think of racism, sexism and other 'isms' as a way of thinking that lives inside individuals: as bad behaviour by immoral people. This way of thinking about oppression is attractive, but profoundly limited. Firstly, individuals do not wake up one day and decide to adopt idiosyncratically racist or sexist views, any more than oppressed groups decide to accept subordinate societal roles. Generally, there is a shared social content to these beliefs: they are remarkably uniform across the population. Secondly, when oppression is codified in rules and hidden in assumptions, it can operate independently of the individual will. Even people who have good intentions can have oppressive effects because they operate within a set of normalised procedures that reproduce power inequalities. Of course, we are morally implicated in how we respond to the system; but the system itself exists independently of our individual ethics.

---

[96] See Johnson (1997, p. 35).

The patterning of power within a society along gendered, raced, abled, or other lines shifts symbolic and material resources to particular groups (men, white, able-bodied) and away from others (women, Black people, disabled people). Anything that either creates such a pattern or perpetuates it whether intended by a person or not is part and parcel of a system of domination and oppression[97].

Our moral sense should be awakened both by our active and passive participation in the reproduction of these patterns. When people who benefit from a power imbalance choose not to disrupt the system, they keep discrimination in place as the 'normal' and unchallenged way to operate a society: they become 'bystanders' to oppression. Whites who do not directly challenge racism and men who are silent about the patriarchy are moral bystanders, and thus complicit in oppression. They help to maintain a society in which oppression can flourish without interruption. Generally speaking, members of groups that are privileged by unequal power systems tend mostly to just "mind their own business" rather than becoming actively involved in direct acts of violence and hostility. These passive oppressors are the silent majority that keep relations of domination in place. They may even distance themselves from their more active fellow-travellers, whose overt sexism/racism/etc. may be disavowed without any harm to the structure of oppression itself.

Oppressive social systems work by affecting the average prosperity of the group. Bad treatment at an individual level may be unjust, and demand a remedy, but unless it is in some way linked to a group-based bias at societal level, it is not part of a system of oppression.

The feminist scholar Iris Marion Young[98] has argued that for a social group to be regarded as 'oppressed', one or more of the following conditions need to be in place:

> **Exploitation**: A group is oppressed if the value of its labour is systematically transferred into benefits that accrue mostly to another social group. In racial states such as the United States and South Africa this dynamic sees huge transfers of value to white people from everybody else. All around the world, the value of women's labour is routinely transferred to men.

> **Marginalisation**: A social group is oppressed if its members are largely confined to the edges of mainstream society, with little or no access in practice to the discussions, activities or processes that shape the dominant social order. In much of the modern world, the most profoundly marginalised groups tend to be indigenous First Nations, disabled people, and people living in poverty.

---

[97] See Johnson (1997, p. 112).
[98] For the full description of the "Five faces of oppression" and the way they are linked to specific social groups, see Young (2000).

Powerlessness: A social group can be described as oppressed if its members by and large do not have the authority formally or in practice to make major decisions that impact on their lives and are frequently at the mercy of others' decision-making. Most transgender people around the world, for example, despite recent advances in specific territories, are disempowered by society at the everyday level of dress, access to space, and identification.

Cultural Imperialism: A social group is oppressed if no value is attached to its actual self-expression, while value may be attached to distorted representations imposed on its self-expression by a dominant group. When a dominant group's experiences, values and tastes are treated as the only important norm, other cultures are systematically treated as invisible, while also being stereotyped as 'exotic' or 'different'.

Violence: A social group is oppressed if attacks on its members whether on their person or their property is seen as probable, inevitable, and 'normal'. This is exactly the kind of phenomenon that the Black Lives Matter movement in the United States (and increasingly in other parts of the world) opposes and undermines. On-going male violence against women and children in South Africa (and elsewhere) is also a prime example of this. The oppressed group typically has little recourse to self-protection, and other groups systematically respond to such violence with complicity, silence, indifference, or justification.

Structural oppression is thus built into the way society works and is maintained not through the direct intention of cruel tyrants, but rather through the conditioned participation of both dominating and dominated groups in upholding the values, assumptions and habits of an unequal system. For oppression to be present, the experience has to be embedded in systematic constraints affecting an entire social group that you are deemed to belong to, and there must be a dominant group that is free from equal constraints and who benefits from the system unfairly.

8.1.3. Reproducing Dominance and Privilege

Our social systems are: *dominated by* privileged groups; *identified with* privileged groups; and *centred on* privileged groups[99]. Let's briefly discuss these concepts in turn.

---

[99] This distinction and the framework for the discussion below are taken from Allan Johnson (1997, pp. 96–112).

Dominance

Privileged groups dominate our social systems by occupying most of the positions of power. However, the exercise of this power is not always experienced as crushing and violent: mostly, it just seems normal and natural for members of these groups to enjoy privilege. For example, in many organisations, the majority of the more senior positions are occupied by men. It is not that men hold *all* the top positions, nor that men don't hold less senior positions too. However, masculinity is still identified with 'what works' in terms of leading an organisation. To have power, it is best to act and behave more or less like a man. And it seems natural and right for men to assume and use power in the organisation, and for others to help them to meet their needs. Men enjoy the benefit of the doubt. When women occupy positions of power in the same system, their behaviour is placed under the microscope: are they taking the lead, are they making tough decisions, are they standing up to the bullies? There is a greater demand on them to prove themselves, and to justify their credentials and abilities. Men in the organisation may feel entitled to question and interrupt them, to insist that they explain themselves, to ignore and disrespect them, to treat them as children, to comment on their attractiveness or sexuality, and to undermine their decisions. These are not behaviours that would be tolerated if they were directed by women towards the men who currently hold the power[100].

Identification

To a greater or lesser extent, everyone is meant to identify with privileged groups. Their characteristics are taken as the aspirational standard for everybody else. For example, in many organisations, the way white people speak and dress and behave are taken as the cultural norm. They are seen as the measuring rod for evaluating how well others are performing. The more an employee can speak English with a typical 'Model C'[101] accent, the more successful and promotable they are seen to be. All the adjectives describing people as having "good manners", being "good with people", or charming, stylish, self-reliant, well-educated, etc., reflect a Western and a white bias. In this way, "well-spoken" simply means "speaking like a white person"; "well-read" means familiarity with Euro/Anglo-American literature; etc. Failure to observe and reproduce the cultural values of the dominant groups become convenient excuses for a lack of inclusion or advancement: people just are not a good 'cultural' fit, are too gauche, too brash, don't connect well with clients, etc. Dominant groups will routinely see the world from an assumed first-person plural perspective ('we' do

---

[100] For excellent and up-to-date parodic materials on societal double standards about women, see the Twitter account called @manwhohasitall, or the book *The Man Who Has It All: A Patronizing Parody of Self-Help Books for Women* (@Manwhohasitall, 2018)

[101] In the South African context, 'Model C' refers to formerly white, English-medium, schools that became multiracial after apartheid.

things like this; 'we' like x, y or z...) while subordinate groups are othered as a strange 'them' whose tastes, habits, and capabilities seem strange and less useful to the organisation.

The point here is that the tastes of the privileged group become associated with success itself: the social norms, cultural production, language use, and consumer choices of the privileged become the aspirational choices for everybody else. Typically, it is the role of marketers to reproduce this skewed picture of society. You generally can't expect to occupy a privileged social position unless you drive the right car and buy your groceries from the correct store. But you also need competitiveness, emotional detachment, assertiveness, decisiveness, and the will to control others. Subordinate value is attached to caring, including, enquiring, nurturing, cooperation, emotional sensitivity, and compassion, where it is necessary to keep the over-arching power system in place.

Centring

Privileged groups expect to see their experience of the world affirmed as normal and good in their everyday interactions with people. They receive more attention and take up more time in educational and other settings. Their experiences are understood and assumed to be of interest to everybody. On the other hand, "women's literature," "Black history" and "lesbian films" are assumed to be of interest only to others in the same social category. Furthermore, distracting attention away from the privileged groups can be met with considerable resistance. When all the participants in a workshop are deliberately given an equal chance to speak, members of privileged groups may ironically feel that they have been marginalised and silenced. Relative to their 'normal' centrality, of course, it is true that their voice has been reduced. Members of dominant groups even report that the experience is traumatic, discomforting, or unbearable, and they may withdraw, or find it impossible to listen quietly for that long or challenge the process (all of which re-centres the attention on them). In dealing with the centrality of privilege in our social systems, members of subordinate groups often find themselves in a double bind. It is much safer to take the "path of least resistance" and remain relatively invisible. When you try to challenge oppressive social relations, you call attention to yourself, put yourself at the centre, and run the risk being accused of having a chip on your shoulder, of being angry or aggressive, seeking special treatment, or just being a general "trouble causer".

8.1.4. Reproducing Oppression Through Internalisation

The preceding discussion shifted the focus from discrimination as a thing that morally problematic people do intentionally, to an analysis of how power relations are reproduced in everyday social interactions, intentionally or not; in short, how they inhere in the social systems. The sad thing about the way that these systems work is that it is also possible for them to be reproduced by the people who are on the losing end of the system: whiteness, for example, demands work of Black people to maintain; just as the patriarchy depends on women's work.

To be clear: there is no chicken and no egg; no one-way causal story to be told. Apartheid as a system, for example, was designed by individual racists, relied on a general level of white racism in society to be made law, and then on everyday people acting in a racist way in order for it to work. But the system also produced the people. So, apartheid was made by racists, but it was sustained by people who were racialised by it. How could that happen?

People from both privileged and oppressed groups often adopt the paths of least resistance in the systems they find themselves in. This does not mean that this path is easy, only that it is has less violent consequences if you follow it than if you try to go a different way. These are ways of behaving for self-preservation, self-advancement, or out of habit that don't rock the boat, and thereby help to keep the systems of privilege and oppression in place. Oppressive systems that become 'hegemonic' do so by being able to present themselves as common sense: It is natural that Europe should guide Africa's development! It is natural that a man should be the head of the household! It is natural that heterosexual families should be at the centre of society! And so on.

Oppression does not always reproduce itself in very dramatic ways; it is often engrained in the most banal social interactions. To the extent that members of privileged groups enact their privilege, they are more likely, for instance, to offer their opinion on an issue they don't know much about, because this is an authoritative was of behaving. The term "mansplaining" has been defined as the "intersection between overconfidence and cluelessness"[102]. In our work, it is not unusual to come across white people who try to explain to Black people what apartheid was really about, or middle class people who want to explain what it means to grow up poor.

People who are dominated by unfair social systems may often find that it makes life more bearable to react with patience and humility to being slighted or belittled. They may come to buy into the idea that actually the dominant groups are better leaders, more intelligent and subtle thinkers, and have deserved their elevated place in society. As Steve Biko famously said, "the mind of the oppressed is the most potent weapon in the hands of the oppressor"[103]. (Biko, 1978/2006, p. 68). "Internalised oppression" does however not just function in a meek and unchallenging way. When members of dominated groups are promoted, rewarded, or celebrated by unjust systems they may attribute their success to the own hard work and determination, rather than to the strategic example being made of their exceptionalism to prove the 'rule' that the system is in fact a just one. The one woman on the senior executive team might thus be complicit both in denying that a culture of sexism exists, and in reproducing the idea that most women are in fact not cut out for rising through the

---

[102] As per Rebecca Solnit's classic essay, "Men Explain Things to Me" (2012)
[103] See "I Write What I Like" (Biko, 1978/2006, p. 168).

ranks as she has, precisely because she has been so traumatised and beaten into shape by the system. In racial states, successful Black businesspeople are often the foremost advocates of the fundamental fairness of the market order and might attribute unequal financial outcomes at a racial level to a tendency to complain and cheat their way out of the system, rather than to any unfair racial or class structure. In the South African context, the legacies of centuries of trauma have had such complex outcomes that we deal with a myriad of intricately interwoven symptoms on a daily basis[104].

Feminist theory offers some definitions of "internalised oppression" and "internalised dominance" [105]:

> **Internalised Oppression** describes the phenomenon of individuals who are members of an oppressed group but that accept the prejudices that are held against them within the dominant society. It may involve a degree of self-hatred, self-concealment, and fear of violence, as well as feelings of inferiority, resignation, isolation, powerlessness, and gratefulness for being allowed to survive. Internalised oppression perpetuates inequality by building subservience into the minds of oppressed groups.

> **Internalised Domination** happens when individuals in a dominant group accept and incorporate the prejudices held against others. It typically involves feelings of superiority, normalcy and self-righteousness, together with guilt, fear, projection, denial of reality, and alienation from one's body and from nature. Internalised domination teaches members of privileged groups that they are justified to have more power than others. It restricts dominant group members' sense of humanity, empathy, trust, love, and openness to others.

These dynamics may emerge in different contexts and in different ways, which cleave to various dimensions of difference. The performance of these relations may also differ from generation to generation, and undergo periods of renewal or renovation. They have also been shown to be supported by a specific range of behaviours, some of which have been described by the American anti-racist psychologist Valerie Batts. In the example of racist orders where white people are raised as if they belonged to a dominant group, the following behaviours may be apparent[106]:

---

[104] See Christo Nel's "Transformation without sacrifice" (2010)

[105] The definitions we use here are from Gail Pheterson's classic paper, "Alliances between Women: Overcoming Internalized Oppression and Internalized Domination" (1986, p. 148)

[106] This version of Batts' descriptions was developed in a paper with Mary Sonn, delivered at the American Psychological Association convention (1985).

Dysfunctional Rescuing: to insist on 'helping' Black people in a way that is condescending, patronising and undermines self-reliance. This kind of behaviour is often based on a belief that Black people lack capacity and thus require special treatment to boost their confidence. It is an unhelpful way of helping.

Blaming the Victim: to blame Black people for problems that stem from structural oppression, without any acknowledgement of the systemic causes. For example, blaming Black people in informal settlements for unhygienic living conditions, or thinking that poverty is caused by "having too many children".

Avoidance of Contact: to make no effort to engage with Black people on an equal basis, to keep interactions superficial and avoid any substantial conversation so that there is never a need to really listen to Black peoples' experiences and opinions. This extends to white people avoiding public places or institutional contexts where they might feel 'outnumbered'.

Denial of Differences: to minimise and discount obvious differences between people, including denial of black peoples' experiences of life, and of racism. This kind of behaviour may also manifest in refusing to recognise and include cultural or religious practices that differ from that of the dominant group.

Denying the Political, Historical, Economical, Psychological and Social Significance of Differences: to underestimate and discount the impact that systemic racism has had on generations of Black people, by for example, suggesting that "we are all equal now" or on an even deeper level of denial, to suggest that whites are now the victims of reverse racism.

Similarly, oppressed groups might manifest their internalised oppression through minimising the racial oppression, accepting powerlessness as inevitable or normal, and discounting the effects of systemic racism. Batts refers to this as a kind of "learned helplessness" which includes avoidance of conflict, difficulty expressing anger, and a tendency to turn anger inwards. That both the oppressed and the dominant play a part in sustaining unequal systems should not suggest that there is a symmetrical relationship between the two, making it seem as if the work to be done by privileged and oppressed people is somehow equally hard, and that the responsibility for overcoming oppression is equally shared. This impression obscures the fact of power. While oppressed people can be engaged in their own oppression, the significant imbalances in power, and the fact that they lose out from the imbalance, places both the blame and the responsibility in the laps of the privileged. This is because the effects of internalised oppression close down the scope for action, promoting a range of debilitating experiences[107]:

A. Feeling restricted, tense and ambivalent.

B. Battling low self-esteem, a sense of inferiority, and self-doubt.

C. Strong emotional responses including fear, hopelessness, anger and shame.

D. Relationship challenges resulting from misplaced anger, distrust and rivalry.

E. Strengths such as resilience, generosity, courage, ingenuity and solidarity.

These power imbalances are played out in everyday interactions, as Hussein Abdilahi Bulhan observes:

> When a member of the oppressing group meets a member of the oppressed, the first always acts as a majority; while the latter behaves simply as a minority of one. The former demands more space and privilege; the latter tends to settle for less. The former exudes confidence and a sense of entitlement; the latter betrays self-doubt and readiness to compromise. Consciously and unconsciously, each knows that their personal encounter is also an encounter of two collectives with unequal power.[108]

These "encounters of two collectives with unequal power" leave a great deal under the surface, and easily evoke ambivalence and stress. As a result, they may be subverted into all varieties of escapist behaviours by members of both privileged and oppressed groups, including self-abnegation, as well as self-destructive activities, which in turn are the behaviours that tend to reinforce internalised dominance and oppression. It is only once we squarely address the massive trauma that historical and present subjugation has on dominated social groups, and the warped and cynical effects it has on dominant social groups, that we will be able to move beyond these problematic social hierarchies.

---

[107] This list is taken from an article by the liberation psychologist Geraldine Moane (2003).
[108] This quote is from Bulhan's biography of Frantz Fanon, *Frantz Fanon and the Psychology of Oppression* (1985, p. 123).

8.2. Working with: Whiteness

We spend most of our time in the sessions just dealing with whiteness.

– Busi Dlamini

Race plays contextually specific roles around the world. South Africa's racial state has been through a number of iterations, which we explored above, but throughout the centuries it has tended to produce a powerful form of hegemonic whiteness. Though apartheid also structured religious, gendered, sexualised, and ableist power structures, its lodestar was *race*. Proximity to whiteness was (and remains) proximity to power. Much of the time that whiteness takes up in diversity literacy processes is however spent debating whether or not it can or ought even to be discussed. It is thus worthwhile to build a specific part of the toolkit for unpacking and confronting whiteness as a power structure.

8.2.1. "But We're All Non-Racialists Now!"

The official Rainbow Nation ideology of non-racialism was heralded as the antithesis of apartheid. Instead of our life chances being determined by the colour of the skin, we would be free to pursue our dreams unencumbered by discrimination sanctioned by the long arm of the law. Unfortunately, many people, especially white people, have read this as meaning that we have an excuse to not have to account for race at all in everyday social encounters, nor to have to correct or enact reparations for lingering inequalities. The sociologist Xolela Mangcu[109] suggests that non-racialism, as a post-apartheid worldview, was unable to bring about the social justice it promised because it became an ideology that worked to mask inequality. While nonracialism as a concept may have had liberatory beginnings, it was its appropriation under neoliberalism through notions of 'colour-blindness' that foreclosed actual redress. The very metaphor of the "Rainbow" Nation was thus distorted: as white light is in essence made up of all the other colours of the rainbow, "the fates of all the people of this diverse country were subsumed within the interests of the white population"[110].

Clearly how we define race and racism as well as how we frame both the 'problem' and the 'solution' is itself contested terrain. We use the term 'anti-racism' instead of 'non-racialism' to suggest an approach that actively challenges *racism*, while acknowledging the relevance and validity of *race* as something that deeply affects our identities and experiences.

---

[109] This is an argument he makes in his edited collection, "The colour of our future: does race matter in post-apartheid South Africa?" (2015)

[110] See Melissa Steyn's, *Whiteness in the Rainbow: Experiencing the loss of privilege in South Africa* (2001).

'Non-racialism'-inspired "colour-blindness" is however a very resilient notion, and takes up a lot discursive space in our sessions:

> *Some of them were very proud of the colour-blindness, saying "I'm raising my children not to see colour" and I think that's a very ahistorical view. It is a view that is insensitive to the present... Because colour affects your life, every day. Inequality is written in colour in South Africa and is laid over with race and history.*

– Pierre Brouard

8.2.2. Killing the Conversation

Refusing to talk about the relevance of histories of discrimination in the present is a conversation-killer. There are unequal benefits to shutting down the conversation in this way. Clearly, those whose privileged position in society which they would prefer to be seen as a token of their merit have more invested in leaving the baggage of the past behind. Inviting these people to become part of a critical conversation about what supports their present social position can be difficult. They have a lot riding on the idea that society is now neutral, fair, and structurally just. Otherwise, the moral legitimacy of their relative position is eroded.

Some go even further: to claim that the post-apartheid order is unfairly punitive to white people. These positions are incongruous with the experiences of most South Africans and are contradicted by a basic engagement with the statistics of inequality. Around the world, conservative right-wing and fascist movements specialise in manufacturing a sense of white victimhood. They mine this 'grievance' which amounts to complaining that white supremacy has lost some of its historical legal protections for all of the political mileage they can extract from it. Narratives about white genocides, anti-white bias, and being forced to be 'ashamed' of being white, are typical of this extremist discourse.

In more mainstream white liberal discourses, refusing to talk about the past is one way of resisting the re-negotiation of power in conversational spaces. It undermines Black agency by robbing it of historical context. It places a burden on Black participants to constantly justify their experiences of inequality as if these have emerged out of nowhere. If our processes are ever to be honest and useful and *transformative*, they must therefore involve actual shifts in power *in the discussion itself*.

Bringing into question whether the past should even be discussed centres white peoples' agency in determining what the rules of the game should be and works to protect white comfort. CDL facilitators need to be careful to deal swiftly and decisively with the inevitable opposition. In certain cases, white participants will accept the invitation to listen, to drop their defences against discussing the past, and to fully explore others peoples' sense of outrage and trauma. This can represent a moment of possibility, where shifts in the power to determine the flow of the conversation can change the pattern of groups working to construct their present and a better future. It is thus a crucial gateway to try and keep open.

8.2.3.   The New Victims

The term "white fragility"[111] is used to refer to a specifically white reaction to being confronted with uncomfortable realities about inequality and racism. In most instances, the beneficiaries of racism want to insulate themselves, and to exert their power in order to switch off, change the channel, walk away, or stop engaging, because there is no cultural or socio-economic penalty to avoiding the issue. As a result, many white people have very low tolerance for race-based stress and often show poor emotional competence in dealing with the topic.

> *We spend a lot of time pandering to white people, trying to convince them that they're not victims, that there is no such thing as 'reverse racism'. Lately, I find the white victimhood is more amplified than ever.*

> **– Busi Dlamini**

Even low amounts of race-based stress being asked to consider their role in sustaining racial hierarchies, in perpetrating microaggressions, or in benefiting from unfair structures are experienced as emotionally intolerable and engender extremely defensive reactions. White people may become unreasonably argumentative, lose their tempers, burst into tears, storm out of the room, or refuse to talk further. This is one of the ironies of the anti-racist movement: that because whiteness has now accepted a negative valency for overt racism, any attempt to deal with covert and other forms of racism is interpreted as an existential and demeaning attack on the very souls of white folks.

8.2.4.   The Challenge of Engaging Constructively with Whiteness: Five Lessons

The childlike intensity with which these outbursts are often accompanied speaks to an emotional immaturity in relation to conversations about race. While many racialized people have had to think about race from the cradle, white people are fed comforting discourses in the media and at home that distract them from identifying their race as a key determinant of their social position relative to others. Whiteness comes with

---

[111] This term has been most elaborately developed in the context of the United States by the anti-racist educator Robin DiAngelo (2011, 2012).

social power, but what very often underlies negative reactions to challenging it is not power, but fear:

> *How does one manage white men? Not only their dominance, but their fear. What we've been confronted with again and again is the fear and insecurity that white men are feeling in the system and we can say: "Tough, your time is now over...". But it's hard to play this kind of zero-sum game, rather than thinking through how we include all of us. Whatever my privilege or my kind of centrality or my normativity that affects my own paradigm, the challenge is to think through what is the work that I need to do to support a system of being inclusive, rather than assume that I'm going to be marginalised in the system? So, it's around how do we help one another.*

– Kirsten Klopper

What is required of facilitators is firm but constructive engagement with the fragility of white people in the room. Below, we have crystallised five lessons from our own experiences and those of our contributors.

Lesson 1: Distinguish Racist Intentions from Racialised Effects

Peggy McIntosh, who we quoted earlier, remarked that she "was taught to see racism only in individual acts of meanness, not in invisible systems conferring dominance on my group"[112] Sometimes white people will feel personally attacked when the subject of race comes up because they think of themselves as fair, kind, good human beings who do not engage in nasty behaviour and certainly do not engage in racist nastiness. However, the fact that we are entangled in racist systems means (as we discussed above) that we can be involved in nastiness without actually being in an intentionally nasty mental state.

> *Because suddenly people are calling them out on privilege, they feel attacked, and they think "hey, we are just trying to be nice white people...!" So I would often say in rooms how I don't think people are intentionally malicious. I think sometimes we're unconscious of the impact we have on others. So that's usually my entry into the subject. I know I impact on other people and for the most part I usually don't have malicious intentions. But I am required to raise my consciousness to take responsibility for how other people experience me.*

---

[112] See McIntosh (1988/2011)

So, I think that was a huge part of the engagement to support people in their own thinking, and to push back against their knee-jerk reactions.

– Busi Dlamini

This strategy will require challenging people's binary worldviews, where you are either a good person or a bad person, either a racist or not, and where you fall in these oppositions depends purely on your *intentional* individual conduct. We need to add complexity to this either-or scenario: people can be good moral agents in some aspects of their lives, and yet profoundly harmful to others in other aspects, without even being aware of the harm that they participate in. This applies to all people, but it is especially acute when addressing the beneficiaries of racialised inequality.

Lesson 2: We Produce Society, But Society Also Produces Us

The dialectic relationship between an individual and social systems is also a good place to start with white people. Though it is clear that individual moral agents can affect society, and do so over time, a significant proportion of who we are and how we act is determined by the way we were raised, and the way that our very subjectivities were formed by ideologies, discourses, and our exposure to institutions. This is how society works and does not make any person especially evil. While we do have a responsibility to resist being hailed into unjust systems, we must first recognise that those system are unjust.

I've seen this over and over again in organisations where the whiteness just remains dominant, because almost at a subconscious level the white people trust other white people to get the job done. And they wanna look good, they don't wanna risk giving jobs to someone they don't quite trust, or they're not even willing to acknowledge that they don't trust... So how to break that? Firstly to validate that it's not wrong to share something in common with other people, to share trust, and that you can get the job done pretty quick and pretty painlessly with people you trust. But then to challenge that a narrow definition of trust creates unfairness. It can also lead to better results to get people from different backgrounds working together.

– Jennie Tsekwa

In this lesson, we can affirm that it feels good to work together with people you know from school, whose kids go to the same schools as yours, whose parents live in similar houses to yours, while acknowledging the massively unfair effect that this comfort has on society. Getting uncomfortable (which we will discuss below in §8.3.) becomes a moral imperative once you can see that your comfort makes you complicit in marginalisation and injustice.

Lesson 3: Teaching, Learning, and Listening

A common problem that facilitators face in South African workshops is an imbalance in openness to learn and to listen between white and Black[113] participants. Facilitators report that even Black participants who were initially hostile to the notion of yet *another* diversity intervention tend to leave the workshop saying *"How do I contribute, what do I need to shift in myself in order to be able to support the change that's required?"*. For many white participants, however, conversations about diversity are often processed at a purely theoretical level; they are intellectualised but not internalised. Their attitude is often: *"Ja guys, that was nice, let us know how it works out for you"*[114].

That white people are profoundly ignorant of what Black people have to go through on a daily basis, not least of all in the workplace, can place a large burden on Black people in workshops to assume the role of teachers:

> *The people are usually smart, so I'm not saying it's a cognitive flaw, but often white people are unable to connect the theory of racism to the lived experience. That means Black people do most of the work of demonstrating the daily implications for the organisation. So you'll provide a tool and ask "how does that play out in the workplace?" and send them into groups... And the white people will sit like just looking confused half of the time. So you come to talk it through: "So, when someone is getting interviewed, right, so who normally would be part of that process?" and they describe that. "So, how do you think having three white panellists might be having an impact?" Right? It's literally working through almost blow by blow which for the most part then, yeah, Black people have to do the labour.*

– Busi Dlamini

Privilege, as we explained in §8.1, is being *normal*: for white people, their way of thinking about the world is natural and self-evidently correct, and there are disincentives attached to questioning your own normality, your own moral certainty:

---

[113] In this case, we are not invoking the complexity of the variety of racialized positionalities in South Africa (i.e., discussing the 'Indian' or 'Coloured' roles in a workshop, or racial 'dissidents' of whatever heritage) but instead deploying a strategically monolithic 'Black' identity category that corresponds to a similarly monolithic 'white'. Clearly, this is not the most subtle approach, though it speaks directly to the dynamics we encounter in our workshops.

[114] These reported quotes were contributed by Busi Dlamini.

If you have a conscious sense of your own superiority you don't want to engage with a history that is shameful to people of your colour, so there is a pushing away, a distancing mechanism that is going on there.

– **Pierre Brouard**

At the same time as there are risks for white people, there are risks for Black people in engaging in these conversations. Assuming the role of teachers is difficult and can even be traumatic:

For black South Africans there can be a sense in which bringing the past and that pain into the present is also difficult, and overwhelming. There are some people who don't want to go there it's too painful... [Talking about this] can be retraumatising.

– **Pierre Brouard**

While there is a certain Black-white symmetry in the emotional risks of facing up to racist structure with each other, there is of course not a normative symmetry: Black people should be under no pressure to perform their own experiences of trauma, while it is an essential part of the process that white people are challenged both cognitively and emotionally.

The anti-racist educator Megan Boler [115] has observed that this presents the facilitator with a difficult quandary of deciding how much space to allow for the angry outbursts of white participants who demand to be convinced that racism exists, and thereby hijack the conversation and bully black participants into defending their own experiences of oppression. She grapples with the need to show compassion for the experiences of such privileged participants, while not allowing them to dominate the process or marginalise the emotional work of others in the room. The facilitator needs to develop strategies to balance the energy in these encounters: to allow for Black participants (or facilitators) to offer learning where it is required, without facing a traumatic cross-examination by white participants. Preventing angry denials and interrogations by white people requires making their ignorance clear, and to a certain extent contextualising their ignorance, encouraging them to understand that they are ignorant for solid historical reasons, and not because they are particularly evil people.

Njabulo S. Ndebele has argued that part of living up to the promise of a 'new' South Africa is giving precedence to Black versions of reality: to stories, descriptions, to a new moral universe that truly transcends the apartheid legacy. [116] If the conversation reiterates the same old realities, and leaves everyone feeling comfortable

---

[115] See *Teaching for hope: The ethics of shattering worldviews* (Boler, 2013).
[116] See *Iphi'Indlela: Finding our way into the future* (Ndebele, 2000).

in their seats, then it hasn't addressed the core question of human agency in transformation. What feels 'normal' will not lead us deeper into transformation, because what feels normal is the shape of the past.

The challenge, therefore, in conversations about transformation, taking place in the complex present, is to find ways of shifting the familiar, of changing what feels normal and appropriate. This requires from white participants a willingness to "step into deep incompetence and ignorance"[117], an unknown zone where they won't know how to behave and interact, and where nothing feels normal. Inviting them into this 'unsafe' but profoundly productive space is one of the key achievements of a successful facilitator.

Lesson 4: A Future Without Hegemonic Whiteness

Can we imagine a future where whiteness is not hegemonic? South Africa experienced centuries of socially engineered white supremacy. While understanding how this structures social life in the present is essential to the process of transformation, so is linking current action to its dissolution in the future. Because of the level of white emotional immaturity, and because of white fragility, it needs to be said that a future without whiteness is not a future without light-skinned people. Pushing back against 'whiteness' means undoing a power structure that reads people as belonging to racialised groups whose values are determined by their proximity to a light-skinned, European, Western 'ideal' type.

Clarifying this, and the extent to which conversations about the future potentially reproduce existing power relations unless we consciously expand our imaginations of the worlds we can build together, is a central and powerful strategy for advancing imaginaries beyond race. The past is always already in the room, whether it has been invited in or not. Focusing the attention of participants on a future that makes a clean break from the present without losing sight of power relations in the present is an important tool in addressing whiteness in the room.

Lesson 5: Works in Progress

A final lesson is that our workshops should not be the entire journey for white people or for anybody else, for that matter. Sometimes it is the occasional insight or a narrow but life-changing epiphany caused by exposure to a specific concept that has the most lingering effects for people. The real work will happen outside of the room, as people start to implement ideas they have learned, new literacies they have developed, in their everyday lives. It is unreasonable to expect the transformation to happen there and then.

---

[117] From *Transformation without sacrifice* (Nel, 2010, p. 29).

One of the people in the group was a white lecturer who said that the ideas that we discussed in the group gave her different ways to engage with her students in class. So, for example there were a couple of Black students who challenged her in a lecture on how a white person could have an opinion on an issue of specific relevance to Black communities. She was able to unpack her own privilege in the class she both owned her privilege and discussed her moral responsibility to do something about it and said that this greatly improved her practice and student engagement.

– Pierre Brouard

The universality of prejudice is not something that can be 'solved'[118] and the same can be said of our histories. Instead of trying to solve the past, we can recognise it. It is possible to be less evasive and defensive. We can become more acutely aware of how the past shapes the present. It is in our power to decide if we are in fact interested in one another's stories. Transformation requires this basic humanity.

8.2.5. White Facilitators

A final point on whiteness is that white facilitators and anti-racists need to think carefully through their own positions and motivation for being involved in the work of building critical diversity literacy in the first place. White facilitators who present themselves as "the finished item" are in fact working against the key insights of the model.

I was marinated in a racist system and I can't today in 2018 say I'm completely not racist. It's simply impossible to say that. So much of that racist system and ideology got wired into me. And my approach to the rest of my life is to do the re-wiring.

– Pierre Brouard

White facilitators and diversity practitioners remain imbricated and implicated in existing systems of domination whether they like it or not. A useful attitude toward this state of affairs is heightened awareness, rather than an affected transcendence.

---

[118] See Nel (Nel, 2010, pp. 30–31)

8.3. Working with: Resistance to Emotional Work

Many of the organisations that we do our work in will have been to a greater or lesser extent constructed along the cultural lines we outlined in Chapter 3: as places where rationality, logic, and the centrality of the heterosexual cisgendered white man has never really been challenged. These masculinist and logocentric assumptions will often be hostile to the idea that what we fundamentally need to do in order to improve organisational life is to do emotional work. Emotions are often constructed as OK if they relate to passion for the brand, but when we talk about 'work' we also talk about facing up to difficult emotions and doing so in the context of having very difficult conversations with each other.

As long as emotions are consigned to the status of "outbursts" and participants are expected to limit their contributions to the "facts" it will be hard to have a serious conversation about oppression and domination in organisational contexts. As long as participants hold the view that emotions "cloud our judgment" we cannot really begin to address the ways in which our emotions and our cognition rely on each other to make sense of the social world, including our places in organisational life.

The clear dividing line between thinking and feeling has been shown time and again to be an imaginary one, and one (as we discussed in previous chapters) that reproduces hierarchies linked to gender, race, ability, and sexuality. The very idea of leadership reproduced in popular culture (and management textbooks) of the level-headed and not too emotionally expressive stable 'adult' who is not like the rash and hot-blooded or excitable 'child' has worked historically to make women, queer people, and people not connected to a particular Euro-American definition of 'white', seem less valuable as leaders. As the feminist sociolinguist Debbie Cameron points out in a recent blog post, the men who describe how the former president of the United Kingdom's Supreme Court Lady Brenda Hale used to "relentlessly pursue her agenda" was couched in language that suggests she is a "an obsessive, a nag and a bully" [119]. Exactly the same behaviour from a man is seen as reflecting the commitment and steely perseverance expected from a leader, while from a woman, it is just shows that she is being emotional and unreasonable.

We will now explore some of the ways in which a resistance to emotions in dealing with difference in organizational life can be overcome.

8.3.1. Binary Thinking

The reason versus emotion binary is one of those irreducible oppositions: [120] white/black, man/woman, good/bad, relevant/irrelevant that harmfully structure our

---

[119] See *Gentlemanly Sexism* (Cameron, 2020)
[120] See the seminal discussions of this divisions in Audre Lorde's *Sister Outsider* (1984/2007b, p. 115) and Patricia Hill Collins's *What's Going On? Black Feminist Thought and the Politics of Postmodernism* (2000, p. 60).

world. This kind of division of the world squeezes out the available room for ambiguity, contrast, and nuance. As the Black feminist scholar Audrey Lorde argues, the foundations for oppression are laid in binary thinking, as it inevitably tilts the attachment of value to one side of the opposition.

When starting to work with organisations, we might be told that bosses do not see the point of "getting all emotional with each other" and want to avoid "whipping up feelings" at all costs. The implication is that peoples' feelings about transformation are likely to derail the process, which should instead be managed in a predictable, time-bound, tidy, reliable, and results-driven way. The proposed solution keeps a lid on the emotional "side". What they end up with, unsurprisingly, is a process that reproduces the status quo.

As diversity practitioners we need to assert clearly and without compromise: it is *impossible* to engage in transformational change without doing the emotional work it requires.

8.3.2. Moving Outside of 'Safe Spaces'

For transformation to happen, we need to allow for cracks that cause discomfort; some educational scholars refer to this as a "pedagogy of discomfort." [121] In pedagogies of discomfort, our banal, routine participation in systems of oppression are purposefully brought to consciousness, leading us to question the deeply embedded emotional patterns that structure our worlds. Gaining an awareness of our own implications in systems of oppression can result in strong emotions. We might feel anger, confusion, guilt, shame, or feel moved to deny that this has anything to do with us. Acknowledging and processing these emotions, working with them in the context of facilitation, is part of the central work of organisational change that needs to be done. Not doing so will merely leave the structure of existing hegemonic discourses in place, as these produce the comfort of the dominant groups. Getting uncomfortable and feeling a bit emotionally vulnerable in the facilitation process is an important part of unlearning the everyday ways that domination and injustice are legitimised in our existing social systems.

Danya Davis and Melissa Steyn challenge the common assumption that anti-racism work or diversity education must be conducted in a "safe environment." [122] Many educators feel that it is important to let people feel safe before they open up, and that transformational processes are best built on the backs of stable and calm engagements. But what 'safe' and 'normal' is unfortunately also often congruent with prevailing social norms. A feeling of safety can rely on old and established ways of

---

[121] Boler and Zembylas (2003, p. 111).
[122] See "Teaching social justice: Reframing some common pedagogical assumptions" (Davis & Steyn, 2012).

thinking and interacting, and merely reproduce the familiar hierarchies that everyone knows so well.

When everybody feels equally entitled to 'safety', the powerful are protected and the status quo is reproduced. People who are on the receiving end of oppression and marginalization will know that it is *unsafe* for them to challenge dominant power structures. To talk about privilege causes discomfort for the privileged and prioritising their "safety" thus works against the pedagogical aim. Facilitators thus need to maintain a fine balance between encouraging dialogue and openness and making a space too safe and comfortable for the beneficiaries of unjust social systems. They should at all costs avoid the false promise of social justice obtained without pain, conflict, discomfort, and challenge[123].

8.3.3. Emotional Inequality

There will be significant differences in the emotional stakes for people sitting in the room when a CDL session is taking place. In the emotional economy of the transformation space, there will be considerable emotional inequality: the chronic trauma of a life of marginalized will be weighed against the acute in-the-room pinch felt by a man who must face their patriarchal inclinations, or the white person who is asked to admit that they participate in the reproduction of a racist system.

Transformation is not meant to leave any of us unchanged. On the contrary, effective social transformation can entail the *shattering* of people's world-views[124]. Admitting the negative impacts of harmful social structures in our own lives can feel especially challenging and emotional. This is true both for dominant groups and those who face discrimination. Admitting that the patriarchy has benefited him might detract from a man's sense of his own achievement, or independence, and our human belief that we have power over our destiny. Discussing the trauma of being exposed to racist, homophobic, or ableist structures can also feel hard: as if we have to deny our own agency and position ourselves as victims in that moment. This emotional work involves moving through disempowerment in an individualistic sense to a re-empowerment that rests on connection and collective transformation.

8.3.4. Becoming Nomads

The critical pedagogues Megan Boler and Michalinos Zembylas suggest that the point of the emotionally hard work of critically appraising treasured aspects of our

---

[123] Discussed in Davis and Steyn (2012, p. 33).
[124] See Megan Boler's essay, "Teaching for hope: The ethics of shattering worldviews" (2013).

supposedly fixed identities is to become "nomads" [125] instead. What do they mean by this?

As discussed, people are in the habit of thinking in binary oppositions. Our whole experience of social interaction involves observing and classifying people in terms of their attributes, conduct, and deficiencies relative to dominant norms and values; everything is coded in terms of conformity and deviation. We develop specific "habits of attention" that produce a sense of equilibrium and emotional wellbeing. We are rewarded by the illusion of a safe and normal world that is the way it is, and in which we can block out those incongruous bits of our experience that sow discord or confusion. If we did not, we would feel permanently discomfort when the differences between ourselves and others were opened for reinterpretation.

Doing the emotional work of transformation involves changing both our "habits of attention" as well as the theories about our place in the world that those habits support. It confronts us with the notion that identity is something that is fluid and malleable and in flux. When people have to give up the idea of a fixed norm that measures your difference from the rest, it can feel like losing your home. They compare the feeling to that of being a migrant, or a refugee. Once you can accept that identity is essentially nomadic that it is shaped by what and who you encounter and will keep changing as you travel through life it becomes necessary to make peace with ambiguity. Living in constant ambiguity means coming to terms with risk and vulnerability, of holding yourself accountable in new ways.

The aim is for each of us to inhabit a more ambiguous sense of self that cannot be reduced to binary positions, while also recognising that we collaborate in constructing the identities of other people. This is as true for participants in transformation processes as it is for facilitators. Discomfort has to be welcomed in and invited to stay; even against our instincts that will try to resolve it and negotiate it away. We need to strengthen our capacity to sit with the discomfort, to let it be amongst us, at least until we can work out what comes next. By increasing our tolerance for ambiguity, we might eventually find ourselves further along the road of self-discovery, hope and community.

8.4. Working with: 'Rainbowism'

In this chapter, and elsewhere in this book, we problematise a specifically South African phenomenon known as 'Rainbowism' [126]. There are however significant parallels to this myth in other contexts around the world. Writing about a parallel idea in the post-Civil Rights United States, Charles Gallagher critiques "color-blind

---

[125] In developing this concept, Boler and Zembylas (2003) bring the critical insights of Uma Narayan (2013) and Stuart Hall (1987) into conversation with the writing of the early 20th Century American philosopher and educational reformer John Dewey.
[126] See "The End of the Rainbow Nation Myth" by Sisonke Msimang (2015).

egalitarianism"[127] as a major hindrance to social progress, and for similar reasons. These kinds of myths are convenient narratives of nation-building intended to get people of all backgrounds working together towards common goals, while working to plaster over the foundations of structural inequality instead of decisively dealing with them. The extent to which CDL, or any other critical pedagogy, ought to produce a different vision of what the future should look like, as an alternative to "post-racial" imaginaries, is still an open question. In this section, we make some very preliminary comments on building a vision for the future that surpasses the "Rainbow Nation" by engaging it constructively.

Taking the nation state as a starting point is, in the first place, a problematic gesture given the struggles of Indigenous people around the world to draw attention to the bloody and colonial roots of most modern states, and South Africa is no exception. And yet the process of 'becoming' a nation in this context does have a certain amount of appeal, as it presents the opportunity for redistributive justice and collaboration between groups differentially affected by the legacies of the past, to secure a new way of thinking the nation that benefits everybody equally. That social vision was hinted at by the group of courageous activists who penned the South African Freedom Charter, describing themselves simply as "black and white together equals, countrymen and brothers"[128]. The (masculinist) "countrymen" of the Freedom Charter are still in some sense an imagined collective, the kernel of a dream that is yet to be crystallised. We stand, therefore, knee-deep in a historical political project, one with a rich past and which now requires of us to reinvent what it means to be "South African". Below, we discuss some ways in which this issue might be addressed in facilitation settings.

8.4.1. The Politics of Belonging

There are many dangers inherent in what the sociologist Nira Yuval-Davis has called the "politics of belonging" [129]. Drawing geographic boundaries around identities necessarily involves separating those who belong from those who do not. Under apartheid, as we know, physical and symbolic boundaries were drawn around ethnic groups. These were presented as irrevocable and fixed, in apartheid pseudoscience, by intrinsic biological characteristics. Racial identity was ascribed at birth and circumscribed the individual's possibilities from that moment until even after their death. This thinking was baked deep into South African social systems over a period of decades.

When in 1994 the racial and ethnic nature of these boundaries was officially revoked, the long-standing idea of identity as innate, and the translation of this identity into narratives of belonging/not belonging, remains pervasive. A national

---

[127] See Gallagher (2015).
[128] Taken from the Freedom Charter (Congress of the People, 1955).
[129] See "Belonging and the politics of belonging" (2006a).

project that is imagined as the absence of race fails to help us imagine how we will surpass race. We are so accustomed to inheriting these pre-ordained identity narratives, that we have little practice in constructing a story of our own.

Yuval-Davis[130] argues that citizenship does not automatically endow citizens with entitlements or a sense of belonging. These dimensions are produced discursively. In the context of CDL training, we need to interrogate the ways in which the production of the nation, nationhood, and/or citizenship potentially work towards shutting down conversations about obligations to people of other nationalities, or indeed to shut down conversations about securing a positive equality between ourselves rather than just preventing the infringement of the rights of citizens.

The politics of belonging in South Africa is constructed in a very specific and even inspiring way in our Constitution, the preamble of which states that "South Africa belongs to all who live in, united in our diversity". According to this assertion, belonging is extended to all who happen to live here, regardless of how they got here or what they've done. This bold statement has unfortunately served more as an aspirational slogan than a reflection of reality: everyone living in South Africa doesn't experience an equivalent sense of belonging or feel particularly *united* with all other South Africans. People express feelings of powerlessness, alienation and invisibility. Instead of feeling united, we are often fragmented and divided "in our diversity". Clearly the political projects that have been used to shape our boundaries of belonging have not gone nearly far enough.

8.4.2. So What Can We Do?

The anti-racist education scholar George Sefa Dei[131] suggests that to fight oppression, we have to start with ourselves. For most of us (i.e., unless we belong to the small minority of straight white able-bodied middle-class men) our own subjective experience already contains the elements of what it feels like to enjoy privilege in some contexts, and to suffer oppression in others. Our own identities are sites of intersectionality and struggle. One of the greatest challenges is not to retreat into what he calls "stable knowledge" the conventional, common sense notions that prop up the status quo. These notions have been produced in a dynamic that involved colonialism and the advocation of a Eurocentric worldview. Part of defining who we are as South Africans involves being brave enough to claim an intellectual and cultural space that isn't dependent upon Euro/American verification or approval. This is not to say that this is why decolonising our schools and universities should never become a technocratic exercise, introducing a few African perspectives into otherwise Eurocentric frameworks. The only way to really challenge the oppression from which

---

[130] In "Belonging and the politics of belonging" (Yuval-Davis, 2006a, p. 207).
[131] See the full argument in his paper "Knowledge and Politics of Social Change: The implication of anti-racism" (1999).

we come, is to actively destabilise the taken-for-grantedness of Eurocentric patterns of thinking; not to contradict for the sake of contradiction, but to seek what Patricia Hill Collins calls alternative epistemologies[132] other ways of seeing the world that have been crafted by people who have been forced to feel as if they don't belong as if they are outsiders to Western modernity.

Forging a new definition of South Africanness is continuous with a practice of citizenship that builds on these alternative epistemologies. We can build these relationships with friends and neighbours, in our families, with classmates and teachers, in the ways we conceive of our workplaces and places of worship, if we think in ways congruent to securing a more just and fair society for all. Maybe in time, as Steven Biko dreamt, "we shall be in a position to bestow on South Africa the greatest possible gift a more human face"[133].

As far as practical suggestions go, the trade unionist James Motlatsi and the industrialist Bobby Godsell have made some suggestions about how to address the dilemma of "building a non-racial future out of the construction materials of a racist past"[134]. They offer two overarching guidelines, which agree with the themes of this book: be honest about our past, be creative and courageous about our future. These are useful suggestions to make to people in positions of privilege and power. The three movements that people can make to begin redefining our experiences of community and citizenship are really relevant only to white people:

Move out of denial and into courageous honesty

Move out of our 'ghettos'

Explore what it means to be African

The point is not to abandon the notion of a Constitutional order, but to make room for all within it:

> *The Constitution that frames our sense of our South Africanness gives some people the impression that the conversation has happened and now we must just move on... people say that's a failure of the Constitution. It absolutely isn't. The Constitution and the Bill of Rights give us the beginnings of an architecture to have those conversations. If you look at LGBT kids in the school sector, 20 years ago it would be unthinkable for a young trans person to say to their teacher no I won't go to the toilet that's been mis-assigned to me. That's now thinkable. Why is that thinkable? It's partly thinkable and*

---

[132] She discusses this concept both in *What's Going On?* (Collins, 2000) and elsewhere in her scholarship.
[133] From Steve Biko's *I Write What I Like* (1978/2006).
[134] From their book *Do It: Every South African's Guide to Making a Difference* (2009, p. 34).

sayable precisely because the Constitution and the Bill of Rights has created an imaginary that I think is very powerful. Now we have to create the spaces to say: well, what lies behind that imagining?

– Melanie Judge

This is the paradox of being *differently* South African, of being like nomads in the unfamiliar land of our common citizenship.

8.5.   Summary and Conclusion

In this chapter, we have surveyed the major obstacles to any critical diversity process: addressing profoundly difficult power structures of privilege, dominance, and oppression; addressing whiteness; encouraging people to have unsafe emotional encounters; and surpassing the Rainbow Nation narrative to think outside of commonly receive stable ideas about what South Africa should be, tied to colonial assumptions. We have offered some tools and guides for how to navigate these difficult topics, mostly at a strategic level. In the next and final chapter, we will review the actions that need to be taken as part of designing specific processes for specific organisations.

Chapter 9

Designing and Leading Courageous Conversations

9.1. Introduction

In this chapter we will first discuss the over-arching issues of engaging with an organisation: the elements to look out for in terms of your strategy of change. In the section after that, we consider the dynamics inside a CDL workshop session. In the final section, we discuss some advice to you as a facilitator about your preparation, personal development, and self-care.

9.2. Reaching Agreement on Programme Design

The conundrum for many diversity practitioners is that by the time we are called in to run an intervention in an organisation, it is already in crisis. Very few organisational leaders are currently farsighted enough to start managing difference productively before it starts to negatively affect their core business. This farsightedness is to be nurtured and affirmed wherever it is found. At the same time, the organisation in crisis represents an opportunity to alleviate the worst symptoms quickly and effectively. The point is that in both scenarios, it is important to keep leadership focused on the long term, and on the thorough-going nature of building critical diversity literacy.

> *People normally call us in at the point of crisis. What I do is to distinguish between what we are going to put in place in terms of what's immediately happening, and what's the long-term sustained change that's needed in the organisation*

> **– Busi Dlamini**

Just because we are engaged in dealing with an emergency does not mean that we should not think through an approach that is truly holistic with an organisation. Even short presentations (as we discussed earlier) can serve as good entry-points to deeper conversations within the team. It is up to us to make the time we have with an organisation as impactful as possible.

9.2.1. Protecting Your Principles

Most facilitators interested in building truly critical approaches to diversity will be departing from a position of social justice activism. As being actively involved in promoting social change is the envisioned 10th principle of critical diversity literacy, there is nothing to shy away from in this position. Organisations, on other hand, especially corporations, but also schools and charities, might encourage a "toned down" approach.

It is important to be firm enough with these organisations to insist that social justice is an integral part of a truly critical approach, while at the same time not jeopardising the opportunity to do the work at all. Change can enter into the system at many different points, and it is important to keep a long view on your relationship: keep your options open, work deeply where you can, try multiple forms of intervention, at different levels. You might not get the opportunity to do everything you would like to with every organisation.

There are so many different paths to change: policies must change; frameworks for managing difference must be adopted; and sometimes, combative confrontation is needed. Some organisations must be taken to court by employees and face direct challenges before they are able to change. Facilitated engagements are very often the injection of a particular set of terms, a particular spirit, the beginnings of a framework, that will affect how the people within the organisation make change happen on their own terms, and on their own turf.

While a workshop on its own may be superficial, and this superficiality is to be avoided, with what time they have the facilitator has the opportunity to focus the conversation on deep issues in the organisation and address complex questions around power and privilege. From the first meeting with the organisation, practitioners should be preparing its members for a deeper, more thorough-going, more lasting change process.

9.2.2. Contracting with Integrity

Many organisations adopt a "Pick 'n Mix" approach to contracting with service providers: they see it as their prerogative to chop and change your intervention. The way you build your big-picture relationship with the organisation you're contracting will set the terms for how much of your integrity and the integrity of your process you can salvage from these important first steps. There are however some broad guidelines that you can keep in mind during the contracting process.

Enrol leaders: Enrolling the leadership of an organisation in promoting your intervention is first prize. If critical diversity literacy is endorsed at the top, at least in its broad outlines, everything else becomes easier. It is good to have a supportive Board member, the positive contact in Human Resources who procured your services in the first place, or an interested stakeholder who promotes your work within the organisation. But the positive engagement of the most senior leaders is profoundly enabling in terms of securing staff time and attention.

Enrol champions: The most senior leadership of an organisation, depending on its size, is not always the day-to-day energy behind making your process work. Getting to know the organisation you are working with and finding people who can drive positive change on a daily basis, is also a crucially important part of contracting. They will also continue to drive change and have crucial conversations after you have left, which is a crucial element of the sustainability of the intervention.

> *I believe in supporting people through the process, but also in developing mentors, champions, that can be go-to people to keep the work going. Here at the University of Pretoria we have discussion groups that are up and running here... those things sustain the work as well and wire it into the DNA of the institution.*

> **– Pierre Brouard**

Don't put all your eggs in the HR basket: It's important to enrol leaders and to enrol champions, but be wary if all of the senior support you have is located in human resources.

> *HR are seen as the 'people' people, but that is a big trap to fall in. To think that HR is the solution, even if they sit on EXCO, they don't actually have much ability to change the day-to-day interactions in the teams. They're not closely enough involved. They become the listening ear that everyone vents to, or the one labour disputes are reported to but they are very seldom actually on the ground. They're actually limited in terms of how much they can change the culture if it's a really unhealthy place.*

> **– Jennie Tsekwa**

Tailor to the team: Though the social dynamics of a country like South Africa create similar organisational dynamics across vast geographic spaces, a one-size-fits-all approach does not take into account where different teams are in their development and in their engagement with each other. Furthermore, schools are different from universities, and corporates different from non-profit organisations. There are many organisations and institutions, with vastly different needs and profiles, so ensure that your process truly addresses them.

I spend a lot of time getting a sense of what would be useful for people and being very clear about that. Unless you are clear about that, both with the people you contract with but also with the entire team, then you really are just running a one-time event.

– Busi Dlamini

Manage expectations: Especially in a crisis, it is important to position yourself and your intervention not as a fire extinguisher or magic wand, but as a capacity-building intervention to install a new dynamism around dealing with difference. Building critical literacy doesn't flip a switch that solves problems: it builds the vocabulary and mental models for people to work through problems themselves. This is an important distinction for your stakeholders on the inside of an organisation to be able to articulate clearly.

Join the dots: If champions and leaders support the outcomes and impacts they can expect from your intervention, they may still need guidance on how the activities that you plan to implement deliver the results you have described for them. Because our sessions are often emotionally challenging (see §8.3) and uncomfortable, managers might be hesitant to expose staff, or teachers hesitant to expose learners, to any potential discomfort. You may need to explain that different versions of the exercises and sessions have potentially different impacts, which all affect the efficacy of the intervention on the organisation.

After we explained it to them, the client said to us: don't do the Privilege Walk. Eventually, we convinced them to go with a modified version, which doesn't have the same impact. So sometimes it's one step forward, one step back... We are flexible, and where we can we modify, but we know where we can't, and we don't. That's always the tension we sit with.

– Kirsten Klopper

These tactics for coming up with a good contract, and for building a firm foundation in an organisation, support the development of the whole process, which we explore in the next six sections.

9.2.3.   Measurement and Evaluation

Where possible, include diagnostic interviews or surveys in your process, as well as follow-up measurements to establish whether or not the intervention has managed to meet all or some of its projected impacts. Of course, the intervention is not a magic wand to immediately transform an organisation. Knowledge levels about power and privilege, and the reproduction of specific scripts about the past, change, society, difference, and responsibility [135] offer compelling and measurable evidence of the progress needed, and the progress made toward, a critical diversity-literate organisation.

> *Organisations will say, 'Oh well we had a climate survey done by someone else like two years ago...' and that stuff is interesting, and it can shed some light on what's going on, but we need to go a bit deeper than others do, to get to the organisational culture as a whole. We need to get to the underlying dynamics that are giving rise to diversity related challenges. Our research gives them a new way of seeing themselves, and we can highlight some aspects of their culture that they are not actually thinking about because of the kind of headspace they operate in.*

> – **Haley McEwen**

The over-arching purpose of these measurement exercises is to hold up a mirror to the organisation, to show leadership what is going on, a diagnostic that points to root causes as well as symptoms. Once the picture in the mirror becomes clearer, you can work together with leadership to measure progress against it.

The essential points to conduct surveys or interviews are of course before the intervention and then after it; how long after, however, will depend to a large extent on the kind of relationship you build with the organisation. Following up over a longer period, and over an extended series of interventions, would be particularly useful for creating the maximum chance of change. Evaluating individual sessions you run is of course also a crucially important part of improving your practice as a facilitator.

9.2.4. Negotiating Time

One of the biggest obstacles to implementing a diversity literacy intervention will be the availability of team members. The urgency of making difference work for an organisation is not always appreciated equally across levels of management, and even when it is, the exigencies of daily work will tend to get in the way of the kind of reflective space needed to really dig deep with a qualified diversity practitioner.

While no facilitator is going to have unlimited time and get exactly the kinds of allocations they want a good thing to aim for at least is that the allocation of time by the organisation is clear, and that they have agreed to a finite process during which

---

[135] Three of us have recently proposed a diagnostic tool for measuring critical diversity literacy in organisations (Steyn et al., 2018).

they will actually give that time. They have to agree that they want to be in the workshop, preferably with attendance stipulated as mandatory for the team members who are supposed to be there. The best scenario would be for the team to congregate somewhere away from their place of work, where they will not be interrupted by meetings and phones.

Often, you will simply have to work with the time that is given you. It can be extremely frustrating to work within these kinds of environments, but at the same time it shifts the emphasis onto process design to get the most out of, for example, a 3-hour meeting, when you might be used to managing a 2-day retreat.

9.2.5. Action Planning

For any engagement with an organisation deeper than an initial presentation, consider making time for action planning. Though the effects of building critical literacy are neither linear nor easily predictable, keeping the attention of the members of an organisation focused on the necessity of actually changing the way they operate both in terms of their internal culture and their external relations is an important part of the process.

Action planning is also often the first part of the process to get compromised when time runs out at the end of a workshop. Managing time and expectations effectively so as not short-change the process as leaving out actions inevitably does is another factor for the facilitator to keep in mind.

> *If I'm having a conversation with you about equity and justice, and about where the systems are failing, and we don't have sufficient time to talk actions, it impacts on the integrity of the whole process. This is both a design feature and a sponsor feature: the sponsor has to give sufficient time, and our design has to allow for translating all of this into what it actually means for our institution. What actions are we going to take? How are we going to apply this? What are the skills that are needed? What are the tools that are needed? And if we don't do that, we're compromising our own value, if you like, our own product.*

> **– Kirsten Klopper**

Just having an action planning section is of course not the full specification of what needs to be done. Actions should effectively operationalise what has been learned in the workshop. It is not enough merely to commit to "respect" for one another, for example. How can that respect be operationalised? For example, if the team has mentioned that women are always asked to take the minutes of meetings, will the team agree that from now on they will ensure that men will take the minutes? There are of course limits to what the facilitator can do in the room. The idea is to try to keep the team focused on generating tangible, measurable actions items, rather than vague commitments to be better people who are nice to each other.

9.2.6. Group Composition

When designing the intervention, you will need to negotiate with the organisation how to select whom will be part of your intervention, and into what groups they will be divided. There are of course a number of options: dividing people by function, by management layer, by division, or by some other factor. You might also face the question: do we divide people by race, or by gender? Is there space for the Black women to have their own workshop? Or the white men? We will address some of these questions below.

In terms of management layer, our experience has been that the more mixed the workshops are, the better. Especially when there is a lot of anger, people will ask: "where are our managers, they need to hear this!" At the same time, you need to be acutely aware of the power relations in the room.

> *Managers and leaders very often can't help themselves in terms of their own centrality, and their own dominance: their voice domination. We work with the principal of deep democracy: that every voice matters. How do you ensure voice equity? You have to learn to manage yourself in order to hear the voices that are more silent normally. And as facilitators, part of our job is to make sure that the more silent voices are brought into the room and that those who dominate learn to self-manage. And that of course is a challenge when you have strong voices in the room. And maybe people in management just want to speak; but when they speak, junior staff might feel inhibited to reply. Some of that work should be done pre-workshop: to gauge people's readiness to listen, to let them get stuff off their chests beforehand, and establish what would it take for us to be able to hear and learn from each other in the room.*

> **– Kirsten Klopper**

You might therefore choose to hold smaller group conversations with specific layers of management before bringing them together into one room. But because the dysfunction in the organisation is often by definition relational, the process cannot end there. The crisis arises systematically and relationally between those different dimensions. Dysfunction resides in multiple levels within an organisation, and it requires those layers listening to each other and going through the same process, very often in the same room, for them to be able to hear each other and to move forward.

Given the intense power inequalities along gendered and racial lines in South Africa, and the fact that (as discussed in §8.1. and §8.2.) these power relations really take up a lot of time in workshops, even potentially retraumatising participants in workshops, the question must arise: do we separate people by race and gender when we run workshops?

There are on balance probably more pitfalls in dividing people than in keeping groups mixed. In one scenario that has played out before, facilitators will impose racial or gendered divisions onto groups that are rejected by members of those groups themselves, who do not feel as if they have anything to say to 'their' group that they don't want to say to everyone. In one example, "Indian" members became enraged at being asked to join the "Black" group. Here, the repetition of racist dogmas caused by the imposed division caused more damage than any benefit that could have come from being able to have an 'in-group' conversation.

At the same time, we should open ourselves up to the idea that there are multiple ways in which people may choose to convene. If, in parallel to the process, team members themselves choose to convene around a specific identity and to have their own conversation, this can be a productive step. It could of course also be a power play to derail the process, if for example, it is the existing power structure that is meeting in order to halt the process. As diversity practitioners we should be alert to the risks and opportunities presented by these groupings.

> *If, for example, the white women all want to have their own group, it can lend itself to serving as a platform for the performance of change, with a fall-back into the comfort of similarity. So, I think the general principle is that diversity is good. It's good to have, because the contradictions are good. A certain amount of resistance is helpful, in a way, rather than not. At the same time there are other kinds of processes where it's very important to have Black people talking to Black people in a very focused way. So it depends. But I think the principle is that one has to try and find ways to not reify these sets of differences such that it almost only ever becomes possible to speak certain things in the presence of certain people. Because of course in that moment you assert and there's the fatal error that Blackness is all the same, queerness is all the same, womanness is all the same... of course it's not. It's always overlaid with our own experiences of identity positions.*

> *– Melanie Judge*

In groups that include diverse subject positions, the skilful facilitator would need to remain acutely aware of just how much work is being done by people who come from groups that have been marginalised and historically oppressed. As Audre Lorde poignantly observes:

> Black and Third World people are expected to educate white people as to our humanity. Women are expected to educate men. Lesbians and gay men are expected to educate the heterosexual world. The oppressors maintain their position and evade their responsibility for their own actions. There is a

constant drain of energy which might be better used in redefining ourselves and devising realistic scenarios for altering the present and constructing the future[136].

It is up to the facilitator to attempt to balance these unfair and powerful dynamics in the room: to avoid putting any 'Othered' group on the spot to "educate X as to our humanity" while at the same time undermining the positions of oppressors and forcing them to face responsibility for their actions. The "energy" should not be flowing from marginalised groups towards those who have the power; despondency can be a heavy anchor that stalls the whole process. We will return to the idea of who does the work in §9.3.3.

The fact is that it is very often the power of a personal narrative coming from somebody who knows what oppression feels like that shifts the conversation into more positive territory.

> *People in the room who have experienced exclusion and oppression can 'see' it better they can explain it better. And yet the same people might be completely insensitive to it in other aspects of their life where they occupy a more powerful position. So it is important to bring out that dynamic in the room.*

> **– Haley McEwen**

Just as is the case with management layers, dysfunction exists both in the relations within groups and the relations between them. Getting the mix right then between work that is done on your own, with people like you, and with people who are not like you, should be taken into account in the design of a critical diversity intervention.

> I argue that this work is relational. Privilege is relational, because your white privilege is in relation to the people who are not read as white, or your straight privilege is in relation to queer people. So we are always in relation to power and privilege, in whatever context we're in, and that is a reality we all have to grapple with. The question is how do we do it in a way that is sensitive, and isn't retraumatising.

> **– Pierre Brouard**

---

[136] In "Age, Race, Class, and Sex: Women Redefining Difference" (Lorde, 1984/2007a, p. 115).

9.2.7.   Thinking Through Space

The way that the space of the intervention is selected, constructed, and managed will also have an impact on what will happen during the workshop, so think carefully about how to design space(s) that promotes accountability, ownership, inclusivity, and ownership. People should feel welcome, and invited to contribute, but also be aware that the space for conversation should be held open for everybody.

The circle is a good place to start. Rather than organising chairs in rows or behind desks, in the style of the Western schoolroom or church, organise them so that everybody can see everybody else with no intervening furniture. Meeting in a circle means that nobody is sitting at the 'head'. In the government systems of Botswana, Batswana meet in bakgotla[137] to discuss important community decisions, and these are organised in circles, and reproduce a notion of equal voice in conversation. This is the case despite hierarchical differences that might be in play outside of the individual lekgotla, once you are in the circle everybody may speak. Circles have a way of sharing ownership, but also of representing the on-going and unending nature of dialogue, that it can carry on as long as people need and to, and also that it can be resumed in the future.

The arrangement of the space should thus in some way reflect the premises that you as a facilitator are bringing to the process itself. This includes your arrangement of recording, presentation, and shared creation opportunities. The way you make the physical space constructs the ideological space for participants to occupy in the course of the intervention. The choice of space and the arrangements for the meeting can also be read by participants in the level of effort and investment that the organisation is making.

> *There's inequity even in how the workshops are run, in the way that facilities are allocated to people and processes, as a reflection of what the organisation values... So you go to an executive workshop, and it's a lovely room and the food is great, and I mean those things count. Then for the others, they'll squash you in a room here, and we'll just eat whatever food is available. It really impacts on the message that it conveys to the participants about whether they are valued or not. Be equitable, because that in itself sends a message: all use the same venue, and where possible use a venue that conveys we value you and we value the process.*

– **Kirsten Klopper**

---

[137] See the research report on dialogue in the South African context produced by Pioneers of Change Associates (2006, pp. 16–18).

Decisions about which room, who will be in the room, how it will be organised, and what people will eat, can impact directly on the outcomes of the intervention.

9.2.8. Negotiating Follow-Through

The relationships built with particular organisations and the people who work in them often require on-going communication and follow-up. Very rarely does even a one-off intervention not have some kind of knock-on effect that is important to think through when designing your relationship with the organisation from the beginning.

One aspect to consider is that organisations will almost always need support after the process as envisioned by management. This can either be something practitioners engage in, or that they build into their action planning.

> *It's important to consider that even what looks like a once-off intervention is part of a larger process. You need to think through what support is needed for action, how people are going to hold each other accountable, how they will sustain momentum and continuity, and how they will make reports visible and accessible. How will they continue conversations, or start conversations, or contain conversations? How will they continue doing the hard work around policies, curriculum, and working together? In many cases, coaching support is needed.*

> **– Kirsten Klopper**

Some of the success stories that facilitators share come tinged with worries about hardworking teams who have taken the process seriously and may be headed for burnout. It would not make sense to push a process to a point where people actually start leaving an organisation not because of the persistence of internal diversity issues, but because they have spent all of their energy addressing them. For this reason, many practitioners will make a point of checking in with previous clients down the line.

> *I believe that follow-up is very important; the places where I've had no relationship, it really does feel like it was just an event, and unfortunately, I think that contributes to why things don't change. So I make sure now to contract with people so that I can check in in 6 months' time, or a year, to see what's shifted. I'm not talking about an M&E process, but rather a space for people to debrief about what they've been able to implement or not. That conversation is sometimes part of the meaning-making that's required.*

> **– Busi Dlamini**

After time has passed people's defences often kick back in, and they revert to the old patterns. Without a clear plan for follow-through and debriefing, a critical diversity intervention can become stalled, and the principles of the model will not become embedded within a longer-term view within an institution.

9.3.   Courageous Conversations

Most of our work is simply about talking. There is of course the popular juxtaposition of 'talk' as opposed to 'action'. There is a pervasive belief that talking is so much theoretical wind, while doing is something is far more practical. Talk is associated with the world of theory, of narrative, of hot air, while action is supposedly that which makes real impact and sees strategies coming to fruition. Supposedly, it is action that changes the world, and not just the conversation that leads up to that action.

We should now be able to recognise this as more binary thinking. Acting and talking are far from being opposed to each other: they are in fact inseparable. As most linguists will tell you, humans know how to "do things"[138] with words, which are actions like any other. As much of our social life plays out symbolically, intervening in the problems in that life must also renegotiate and reassemble symbols. We should also be aware that there are gendered dimensions to the binary: woman supposedly like the drawn-out discussions, whereas men are constructed as wanting to get their hands dirty by taking action in the 'real' world.

The point is not to overvalue discussion: we also need action-based change to policies, behaviours, and structures. But these must emerge through a process of creating shared understanding of the organisation, and this happens in dialogue. Our jobs as critical diversity practitioners commit us to a model where we can change the world through talk, facilitating "courageous conversations" that are uncomfortable, but result in real change in the social fabric. In this section, we unpack some of the principles of these courageous conversations.

9.3.1.   Guided Dialogue

Conversation is in fact a form of action: it is incredibly impactful, and so needs to be guided. Conversation is both a precursor to action, and action itself. When we talk and listen differently, we alter our defences and our habits of attention. We shift social norms. The boundaries between Self and Other are affected, and we begin to engender small reworkings of what is possible. It is the conversational experience itself that is foundational in bringing about these shifts.

If people resist conversations about transformation on the basis that "there's been enough talk already", or "what's the point of talking when nothing ever changes" then it's unlikely that they have experienced a truly transformative conversation, or that they fear the power of entering fully into deep and powerful dialogues on subjects that

---

[138] This is the famous thesis of J.L. Austin's (1962) *How to Do Things with Words.*

unsettle them. Such conversations are never going to be easy or pleasant and are a far cry from superficial talk of the Rainbow Nation. They call on us to face our demons, and this is where courage comes in.

In the living system of an organisation, people interact all the time, and sometimes these exchanges may take on the qualities of courageous conversation. But this is usually prevented by our habits of attention, our internalised dominance and oppression. This difficulty generates the need to create intentional spaces where risks can be taken.

The tenor of the conversation needs to avoid *debate* and promote *dialogue*. The Black feminist scholar Patricia Hill Collins points out that a particular mode of Eurocentric thinking posits that "adversarial debates become the preferred method for ascertaining the truth: The arguments that can withstand the greatest assault and survive intact become the strongest truths" [139]. Instead of this epistemological violence, which works to favour the powerful, Collins suggests not that we embrace untruth but that we seek out *dialogue* with others where connections between positions are elaborated, rather than strict conceptual oppositions, a tradition she argues is more closely aligned with the African intellectual tradition [140].

As a mode of enquiry, debate—no matter how expertly facilitated—especially on issues that relate to the humanity of people in the room, risks reproducing an assault on that humanity. As we have seen, these assaults are potentially (re)traumatising to people who have been marginalised. Dialogue instead allows people to hold various views and to consider them without the epistemological violence of "you're wrong" or "you're lying" etc. Dialogue gives space for a number of voices to be heard, and not to be drowned out in the eloquence, volume, or conviction of a more powerful voice in the room.

Dialogue and listening should be protected from debate and lengthy tirades. Facilitators have a number of strategies they use to promote voice equity in dialogue spaces.

> *Finding ways of facilitating voice is of course what is really hard in these processes. You just have to shut certain voices out. Sometimes, you have to shut up the men. I would never call it silencing, but simply sometimes shutting people up. I have developed some active ways of doing this with my body, whether it's gentle gestures, or where I position myself, to try to serve as a corrective obstacle to allow the conversation to flow in a certain way.*

– **Melanie Judge**

---

[139] See her essay "Black Feminist Epistemology" in Collins (2009, p. 274).
[140] See especially the section in the essay entitled "The use of dialogue in assessing knowledge claims" (Collins, 2009, pp. 279–281).

The kinds of talking and listening we do in sessions needs to be qualitatively different from our 'normal' habits of attention. Facilitators must be extremely sensitive to the kinds of communication that is happening in the room. The Canadian social entrepreneur and facilitator Adam Kahane[141] identifies four types of communication that affect the kinds of conversations that end up happening:

> **Downloading** restates what is already known and familiar, where we say what is expected of us, or repeat the same conventional sets of words people usually say. It can be reassuring and cordial to engage in a customary interaction, but it is unlikely to change the world, as it is geared to reinvoke that which is familiar.

> **Debating** involves taking up and defending a position; debate relishes discord and disagreement, which requires locking down fixed and adversarial opinions. Exchange involves inevitable juxtaposition, feeding into a right/wrong binary. Because it calls on participants to reduce the complexity of the world into clear-cut judgements, and therefore has little scope to generate new understanding or relationships.

> **Reflective Dialogue** calls on participants to talk and listen in such a way as to welcome and explore multiple interpretations of reality; they try to see the world through one another's eyes, and become conscious of the limits of their own world view. Assumptions are challenged and a bigger picture, a composite of diverse perspectives, emerges. People make new connections and draw insights from a collective.

> **Generative Dialogue** is a way of communicating that allows a group to discover a shared purpose that emerges from the system they form. People are no longer separate pieces of the puzzle, but are each reflective of the whole. Participants are sensitive to affective connections between them, and allow a kind of clarity, hope, and commitment to emerge.

The facilitator needs to practice voice equity precisely because there are almost always already people in the room who have the critical capacity to take the diversity literacy process forward.

> *There will always be a couple of people in the organisation who are very critical, who've been thinking a lot. They're aware of what's going on they have a critical way of thinking about it and then they speak about that.*

---

[141] In the guide, "Changing the World by How We Talk and Listen" (Kahane, 2002).

That's always great. A lot of our job is just to let people share their views like that, in the kinds of spaces that allow them to talk.

– Haley McEwen

Listening to what comes out of groups is especially important for facilitators. We are often surprised by how seemingly conservative or problematic teams have already implemented quite radical changes in their workplaces, borne of their own experiences. Our own preconceived notions about what groups need or do not need to learn can thus be challenged.

Facilitators set the parameters for what kind of conversation emerges through their own body language, and through the way that they model listening and responding to group members. By actively and consistently listening to the speaker, they convey their interest in them as people, giving them the assurance that what they say and feel is important. Listening communicates trust that the speaker has a valid contribution to make. While this mode of communication to the participants in an organisational change process may well be unspoken, they are crucial to creating the kind of environment where people really are prepared to listen to each other.

Listening, however, does not have to be synonymous with tolerance of all perspectives.

I believe in creating a contained space, and setting very clear terms of engagement, and dealing with the issue of discomfort upfront. We go in with a certain set of underlying principles... There is a broad social contract, with all its imperfections, embodied in the Constitution. And that is the non-negotiable ground that actually has a holding function, a containing function. People should not be allowed to debate whether you really want to see me as human, whether you want to see me as equal... the social justice underpinning is part of an investment in a legitimate, viable, and powerful framework for change. Because without that undergirding, that underpinning principle, it's very hard to run processes.

– Melanie Judge

9.3.2. Applying the Critical Diversity Literacy Framework

In this book we have already advocated extensively for the application of the principles of Critical Diversity Literacy. It is useful to think through these principles in terms of questions that can be tailored to specific groups in specific contexts. Each group is going to have specific dynamics that make the various elements more or less relevant to them, and the idea should always be to tailor the content to the specific group.

Specifically, the framework takes on a different angle in contexts where you are working with people who occupy dominant social positions. When you are working with people who have internalised their own impression, you will need to angle your work with the framework differently. In nearly all contexts, we work with both dominant and oppressed social positionalities at the same time.

Let us discuss a specific group: white South Africans. Some provocative questions that can challenge individuals and groups to reflect on their own level of CDL include:

---

1. Do I understand that "race" was a social construct that emerged historically under conditions of unequal power, in order to justify, reproduce and sustain a racially hierarchical world?

2. To what extent do I accept, and am I comfortable with, a world where is seems normal for white people, overall,

    2.1. To be in charge or organizational spaces?

    2.2. To have more wealth, access to better healthcare, education, etc.?

    2.3. To be unaware of the actual life experiences, struggles of black people?

3. To what extent do I give more credibility to views of white people?

4. How may I be invested in the reproduction of a white-dominated world?

5. Do I make an effort to gain access to, and understanding of, analyses, knowledge, narratives, emotional realities etc. of those I have been raised think of as the "Other"?

6. Do I make an honest attempt to educate myself about our history (including that of the modern world) from a perspective that honours those harmed by colonialism and apartheid?

---

7. Have I equipped myself with a vocabulary and conceptual tools to recognize, name, and engage in dialogue about dialogues about dynamics of privilege and oppression in a specific context?

8. Do I also participate in "white talk" that obscures the racial dimensions of issues, making then "colour blind" rather than exposing and dealing with these racial dynamics?

9. Do I interrupt/disrupt/break rank with attempts to draw me into racial consensus and collusion?

10. Do I try to create environments that are inclusive, safe, enabling and affirming of everybody who has a right to be there?

11. Do I check myself to see why I get triggered or become defensive when certain issues come up? Do I understand how my emotional responses may be related to expectations of privilege?

12. Am I committed to bringing about more socially just arrangements at all levels of society?

These questions can be used to structure different exercises for groups and should be tailored to specific dynamics and histories. While it might be productive to do some probing with certain of these questions in diverse groups, when working with groups in oppressed social positions they need to be significantly reformulated in order to address the specificities of our participation in the unjust social structure. So for example, while discussing Question 8 with white South Africans you may want to shift the conversation with Black South Africans to a deconstruction of colour-blind ideology, and destabilising tactics when "white talk"[142] is encountered. The point is to never fall into the trap of thinking that different social groups somehow bear equal responsibility for addressing these dynamics: the responsibility sits with those who benefit, while those who are harmed clearly have the agency to challenge and dismantle them.

---

[142] See Melissa Steyn's (2005) chapter on "White Talk."

9.3.3.   Invitation to a Discomfort Zone

Nobody wants to be trapped into talking in an unsafe space. But as we have seen above, the creation of a safe space cannot also construct a comfort zone it must be uncomfortable in order for the social order to be critiqued. Normal, everyday life is unsafe for people in marginalised social positions, and the notion that the diversity workshop is magically made 'safe' often masks the way in which powerful people are allowed to get away with indifference to injustice, and disengagement from change processes.

But how does one invite people to share space in these discomfort zones? The educationalists Glenn Singleton and Curtis Linton have recently[143] developed the concept of the courageous conversation in relation specifically to school settings, in which they propose that workshop participants make four commitments in advance:

1. Be willing to **stay engaged**; in other words, emotionally, intellectually, and socially involved in what is being said.

2. Agree to **speak your truth**; be honest and open, and don't just say what you think people what to hear, but speak for yourself and not on behalf *your* social group, but especially and most importantly not for *anybody else's* social group.

3. Be willing to **experience discomfort**; avoid denying it, looking away, getting defensive, trying to smooth things over or 'fix' a heated conversation.

4. **Expect and accept non-closure**; we will not walk out of the room having solved the problem of equality, but we can become more attuned to each other if we stay engaged in the conversation.

So the promise of courageous conversations is not that they will help us to finally solve all our problems so that we can resume our real lives. We are all works in progress and meeting our differences in the spirit of dialogue and equality is a much better starting place than expecting a transformative workshop is going to magically fix all of our problems. In the kinds of societies we come from, the discomfort of transformation will be intimately connected to power inequalities and our emotional attachments to justificatory logics for our own dominance or oppression. Discomfort is sustained by dialogue that scratches at:

---

[143] See their book, *Courageous conversations about race: a field guide for achieving equity in schools* (Singleton & Linton, 2007).

- Internalised dominance and oppression.

- Daily habits of victimhood, superiority, authority, and learned helplessness.

- Our fears about each other.

- Contrasting accounts of the social world linked to our positionalities.

- How what we say in conversation can wound, but also heal.

- How our divisions surface in what is said and what is not said.

Conversational spaces in unequal societies are distorted by imbalances of power. The German political scientist Jürgen Haberrmas famously theorised the space of the "rational public sphere" as the location where public reason is exercised; where we get together to arrive at what works best for all of us. The problem with this notion, as many critical scholars have pointed out, is that our access to this sphere is inflected by relations of domination and oppression: by the very power relations we are trying to escape. In this interpretation, dialogue undistorted by power is no more than a pipe dream[144]. So while we continue to strive to be courageous in the way that we structure conversational spaces, and to reach towards a more just and equal world, the process of getting there is not always calmly rational. Peace and harmony might understandably be impossible to maintain in the CDL workshop space. When we start to scratch at these uncomfortable topics of communication, which go deep into our sense of ourselves, as well as into our organisational lives and notion of ourselves as citizens, the conversation can become a site of great struggle over competing versions of an account of reality. We need to hold the sense that objectively pinning down reality for once and for all is not possible, least of all in the context of a workshop! More broadly speaking, what is often defined as being objective reality eventually boils down to presenting the subjective and narrow perspective of a dominant group as if it were fact. 'Reality' is intimately linked to power.

The facilitator faces the everyday ways in which people assert their power over each other. Those everyday ways are comfortable, they're known, and people derive power and status from them. And that's what we're ultimately here to unpack. So people are invested in low levels of critical diversity

---

[144] For an exploration of this critique in the management sciences, see the organizational development scholar Astrid Kersten's paper "Diversity management: Dialogue, dialectics and diversion" (2000).

literacy precisely because they're invested in certain forms of structural inequality, certain forms of power, certain cultural codes, certain ways of being in the world, certain registers of talking, certain lexicons, certain cultural scriptings.

– Melanie Judge

The facilitator must therefore maintain an acute awareness of how the conversation emphasises groups in the room: is it focusing on those who experience violation and oppression, or on the centre of power? Participation in the "pornography of pain" can leave people comfortable in their positions, both as oppressed and as oppressor. Often, facilitators need to ease people out of their comfortable roles.

Sometimes people perform how aware they are of oppression, which also creates a problematic dynamic. You have a white male who speaks on behalf of everyone, and you can't get him to shut up. And that slows it down a lot, because there's a lot that needs to be expressed, while this person's just busy trying to contain it all, while presenting themselves as being on board with what you're doing.

– Haley McEwen

Getting the balance right between a 'hard' process that challenges people to experience discomfort, but potentially results in disengagement and a 'soft' process that engages people but potentially fails to shift people from dominant modes of thinking is very difficult.

A courageous conversation not only invites but actively encourages its participants to break out of their comfortable structural parameters. When diversity interventions avoid this discomfort, they become part of the problem. These kinds of conversations merely contain and manage social inequality and injustice. Courageous conversations pay serious attention to the *distortion* in the system; they address "the difficulty we have hearing the voice of the Other above the noise of structural inequality, the pain of exclusion, the denial of difference"[145] and the daily impact of living in the claws of a raced, gendered, classed, and ableist ideology that is barely acknowledged by dominant groups. Our work as designers and facilitators of these processes is to work against the ways in which the social grounds of discussion are already prepared to marginalise and invalidate the perspectives of dominated groups. The conversation must actively work against power imbalances, and this will in many cases rely on our own ability to reflect on our subject positions and implications in prevailing systems of inequality.

---

[145] According to Astrid Kersten (2000, p. 237).

One of the things I look out for is whether people view transformation as [being] about loss and pain, or about possibility and opportunity. Those of us who do this kind of work have to be able to speak to both parts at the same time: not privilege one over the other, or focus only on one aspect. I think if you only focus on transformation as something joyful and happy and you don't acknowledge the pain and the loss, then you are missing out on people's actual experiences. But at the same time if you only focus on pain and trauma, then there is this revisiting of trauma [that] can lead to 'stuckness'. You have to be able to say: we hear your trauma, we acknowledge it, we honour it, but we also all want to commit to the possibility of moving beyond it.

– Pierre Brouard

Of course, the extent to which certain groups of people may be open to that possibility will vary along a number of factors, not least of all age. Learners in schools for example might have a more open approach to moving forward than their teachers or their parents. Yet the sad reality is that in South Africa fault lines start getting drawn from a young age. Even seemingly positive and affirming messages, such as the idea that "we're all in this together" can at times seem like it glosses over the problems people face in their daily lives.

9.3.4. Lesson Plans

Lesson plans should combine the didactic elements of critical diversity literacy learning and employing the vocabulary to discuss organisational space with the development of tools and skills that are actor interactive and more practical in nature. The idea is to keep participants intellectually, emotionally, and actively engaged in thinking through the ten principles of critical diversity literacy, and their application in the institutional context.

Different facilitators are going to find different tools and exercises that are best suited to the group, the institution, and their own style as facilitators. It is not our intention in this book to give you explicit instructions on how to construct your sessions; we would rather like to provide the framework, and tips to point you in productive directions in your practice.

These four tips present some of the tools our contributors use in workshops to unlock various aspects of thinking and conversation in their groups:

Tip 1: Use accessible and entertaining learning material to introduce complex topics

In the school work we brought in the Chimamanda Ngozie Adichie video about more than a single story, and we found that a very powerful entrypoint into intersectionality... Because it says that everybody is a complex of many factors: race, gender, class, sexuality, and history, and, we need to see it gives us a chance to move beyond stereotypes and to see those different factors working together to make someone who they are.

*– **Pierre Brouard***

Tip 2: Draw analogies between different forms of oppression to connect with something your participants can relate to from their own identity positions

Sometimes white women will understand whiteness better if you talk about how patriarchy works... the best allies in institutions are often white women who've done some of the work around gender, and have been able to make the connection to race, right? So they enter the work through a gender lens. At the same time, there are white women who will literally finish a sentence about gender discrimination and insist that Black people are being entitled and playing the race card!

*– **Busi Dlamini***

Intersectional thinking is one of the most productive areas to explore. If we only talk about white privilege in certain spaces, it can be a little about immobilising for white people. Sometimes, a Black man, for example, who can speak to his own male privilege, or heterosexual privilege, can reflect on how that interlocks in complex ways with his being Black. So while his Blackness 'others' him, it also counteracts other forms of privilege, or they may intersect in unique ways. There is a danger that this can tend to let white people off the hook a bit as in, 'Oh well, I have white privilege, but you have straight privilege, and class privilege, so we're all good right?' And that would be an unfortunate outcome. But I think if you're a facilitator of that kind of work you have to push back on those sorts of ideas.

*– **Pierre Brouard***

Tip 3: Theoretical concepts and technical terms are not the best entry-points. Rather start with specific scenarios that connect back to real life.

When talking about terminology, you have to unpack it in case studies, and in scenarios. It's one thing to know a definition of racism, but can you spot it when it happens?

– Jennie Tsekwa

I would never go in with terms. I would never start with a term. I would only start with where people are. And if you ask people the simple question of, for example, 'When did you first know you were a boy'? 'At what point did you know you weren't a girl?' If you start to ask those questions and then you can ask, 'When did you know you were a white boy?'. Then you start to get to intersectionality right there from people's experiences... It is about people in their own words understanding what 'hegemonic' or 'dominant' means. Corporate language, NGO language, and certainly academic language sometimes closes the space for that. That's never the entrypoint: the term. So when I say language I mean the language of people's experiences and histories and identities.

– Melanie Judge

Tip 4: Create exercises that give people an immediate sense of inequality and injustice in the context of the workshop

One of the exercises we did in the school was to divide the group into smaller groups of about 4 groups of about 20, and then we gave each of them different kinds of resources to come up with a poster on the transformation of the school. But some of the groups we gave lots of resources to, and some of the groups we have much fewer resources to. And then we observed the process of how they used those resources. When we got them to present their posters, we asked did you notice that you only had black kokis and bit of newspaper, and you had colour and glue and glitter, and then the penny dropped. They got very angry at us!

– Pierre Brouard

There are hundreds of different exercises you could try, and an infinite array of ways to put the workshop together. You can also refer to the WiCDS website[146] to get access to new tools and lesson plans that can be implemented by all practitioners.

---

[146] www.wits.ac.za/wicds.

9.3.5.   Session Outcomes

Courageous conversations must not be allowed to lapse into voyeurism. People expose themselves to each other when they talk about dominance and oppression, and the facilitator's role is to try to steer the conversation towards mobilising people to real action, to social justice practice. As discussed in §9.2.5., that sometimes means actually setting aside the time for action planning. But most of all it is about what the group has experienced together, and the extent to which the process has really 'clicked' for participants.

> *As we got feedback from the group about what they were going to do, I actually got blown away, I thought: this is going to disrupt the organisation. People felt empowered; they were going to say this... they were going to do that... they felt real agency. They were excited about disrupting power dynamics, and relationships systems. It was the most thrilling experience: the sense of agency that people discovered in themselves was so incredible as to be overwhelming.*

> **– Kirsten Klopper**

The power of the process can be quite unpredictable and is not always strictly under the facilitator's control. Because it unleashes the agency of team members, and is not imposed externally on the organisation but arises organically from within it, it is also far more sustainable and impactful. The literacy that is developed is applied by team members themselves to their own experiences and contexts.

> *I've definitely been in workshops over and over again where people have said 'Oh now we can talk about it! Now we can name things!' 'That's exclusion now we have a word for it!' I am frequently blown away to be honest by how intelligent professionals in complex organisations lack the most basic definitions of terms such as race, and racism... When they come up with their responses in the workshop, I was like whoah! So it's really about creating a common language.*

> **– Jennie Tsekwa**

This immense power of the group is channelled appropriately when the facilitator has ably managed the psychodynamic dimensions of the workshop. When these are focused on the kind of generative dialogue discussed above where the humanity of all participants is allowed to give rise to a new sense of what people share as humans rather than a corrosive questioning of people's fundamental value even those who were initially hostile to the process may find themselves experiencing some form of catharsis.

Put 20 people in a room for three or four days and there's a lot of power and possibility in that exchange. There is a new emergence of seeing the Other, literally, in a different way, in a way that is complex, that is not only one thing. When you start to see the Other as a whole person, you see them as bigger than the sum of our sometimes very static analyses of inequality and violence and history. Getting people to think about how power has been enacted on them, in very disciplining and regulatory ways, is very humanising, and opens up new spaces of possibility. We all have an experience of that, even the worst among us.

– Melanie Judge

This is the best we can hope for as facilitators.

9.4.   Facilitator Preparation and Development

Finally, a few words on your own process and preparation are relevant here. It is very easy to get weighed down by the magnitude of social inequality and dysfunctional social relations in organisations. Staying in touch with other practitioners, developing your own practice, and maintaining a routine of self-care are all important aspects of continuing to be a productive part of building critical diversity literacy in whichever context you work.

Where possible, do not work on your own. It can be extremely useful to the process when the practitioners and/or facilitators themselves are a diverse group of people who can speak to a variety of social dynamics and experiences. This establishes a creative tension in experience and approach between two facilitators, so that participants see difference and dialogue in action even between the facilitators.

Facilitators should do their homework about the organisation they are going to engage with. What do you know about the organisation and its purpose, its internal culture, the people that will attend the workshop, their backgrounds, and what you sense are the key drivers of the behaviours? When preparing, you can select language and examples that are familiar with them, in a way that forestalls overwhelming opposition. If you start presenting and people are not convinced that you are authoritative on either their organisation or on the subject material of critical diversity literacy, it can serve as a significant hurdle to an effective process.

Every group is going to present its own complexities: intellectual, emotional, and historical complexities, complexities that come up in the room in the moment. Being properly prepared for this (which of course becomes easier with experience) means that you will be better able to hold the complexity in the moment without trying to either solve it, or push it to one side.

Most importantly, getting better at this involves doing diversity work in your own life. If you as a facilitator have reached the conclusion that you are fixed that you are no longer a work in progress but a finished product it might be time to consider moving on. Nobody has all of the answers. We all have demons to face. What agency can we develop in our own lives? What action can we take in the world to reduce inequality and injustice? What's the meaning we're hoping to assign our group or individual identity? We are all in the process of unlearning our own oppression, our own dominance.

We are unavoidably caught up in what happens in the sessions. Our own identities are interpolated, and this is specifically where having a co-facilitator can come in useful.

White facilitators in particular must reflect carefully on the ways they engage in processes of learning and unlearning racial scripts. Colleagues can learn a lot from debriefing with each other and talking through what worked or didn't in aspects of the other's practice.

> *I am a strong believer in peer supervision. How do we process the trauma that we pick up in systems, and our own experience of trauma and challenge? Black facilitators experience racism, so what is my role as a white facilitator in supporting Black facilitators? My own learning has been primarily through learning and hearing from the experience of Black people not at their expense, I hope. But I also have my own experience of internalised oppression, which has given me empathy and understanding of the experience of marginalisation.*

> **– Kirsten Klopper**

Black facilitators, women facilitators, queer facilitators, disabled facilitators, will come under attack either directly or covertly in spaces they are supposed to 'control'. At the same time as these attacks can be painful, they are an indicator that you as a facilitator are still participating as a social equal in the dialogue.

> *The challenge and the pain in the moment is real. And it has to be. If you're not feeling pain in that, it means you've elevated yourself above the people you're working with, and that's where the judgment can creep in. So you have to remain humble. You have to remain humble, you have to remain in a learning mode yourself. And you have to create spaces for reflection. Otherwise and I'm saying this very much cause I've been there many times... as practitioners we will get triggered. We have to constantly be self-reflective. What are my triggers, how much of my own personal story do I share or not share? And do I have people around me who can also show me my blind spots, am I co-facilitating with someone who can give me feedback when I overstep?*

> **– Jennie Tsekwa**

Many facilitators refer to the necessity of some kind of 'spiritual' discipline which could be quiet time or meditation for some people, prayer for others, or time in nature for others that gets you out of the social space from time to time. Something that centres you, and grounds you, outside of the context of the people you work with professionally. This kind of practice can be extremely helpful in avoiding burnout.

9.5. Conclusion

In this chapter, we started by describing the process of contracting with the organisation, defining the eight over-arching things to look out for in the process. We then got down to the nitty-gritty of running workshops: the courageous conversations that serve as forms of dialogue, specific questions to build critical diversity literacy, the creation of 'discomfort zones' and how to structure them in relation to specific tactics and outcomes that support the impact and sustainability of critical diversity literacy. In the final section, we offered some guidance on things you should do for yourself as a facilitator both to improve your practice, and to maintain your mental and emotional health.

At this point, we can only wish you every strength and the best of luck in your work transforming organisations. Step by step and piece by piece, you will be an important part of building a better world.

Bibliography

Acker, J. (2004). Gender, Capitalism and Globalization, Gender, Capitalism and Globalization. *Critical Sociology*, *30*(1), 17–41. https://doi.org/10.1163/156916304322981668

Acker, J. (2006). Inequality Regimes: Gender, Class, and Race in Organizations. *Gender & Society*, *20*(4), 441–464. https://doi.org/10.1177/0891243206289499

Ahmed, S. (2001). The organisation of hate. *Law and Critique*, *12*(3), 345–365.

Ahmed, S. (2004). *The cultural politics of emotion*. Edinburgh: Edinburgh University Press.

Ahmed, S. (2007). The language of diversity. *Ethnic and Racial Studies*, *30*(2), 235–256. https://doi.org/10.1080/01419870601143927

Ahmed, S. (2012). *On Being Included: Racism and Diversity in Institutional Life*. Durham, NC and London, UK: Duke University Press.

Ahmed, S., & Swan, E. (2006). Doing Diversity. *Policy Futures in Education*, *4*(2), 96–100. https://doi.org/10.2304/pfie.2006.4.2.96

Alcoff, L. (1991). The Problem of Speaking for Others. *Cultural Critique*, (20), 5. https://doi.org/10.2307/1354221

Althusser, L. (1967). Contradiction and overdetermination. *New Left Review*, *0*(41), 15–35.

Baker, A. (2014). *Shaping the developing world: The West, the South, and the natural world*. Los Angeles, CA: CQ Press.

Bekker, S., & Leildé, A. (2003). Is multiculturalism a workable policy in South Africa. *International Journal on Multicultural Societies*, *5*(2), 121–136.

Berry, E. C. (2007). The ideology of diversity and the distribution of organizational resources: Evidence from three US field sites. *Annual Meeting of the American Sociological Association, New York, NY*. Presented at the Annual Meeting of the American Sociological Association, New York, NY.

Biko, S. (2006). *Steve Biko 'I write what I like': A selection of his writings*. Johannesburg: Picador Africa. (Original work published 1978)

Bilimoria, D., Joy, S., & Liang, X. (2008). Breaking barriers and creating inclusiveness: Lessons of organizational transformation to advance women faculty in academic science and engineering. *Human Resource Management*, *47*(3), 423–441. https://doi.org/10.1002/hrm.20225

Block, P. (2008). *Community: The Structure of Belonging*. Oakland, CA: Berrett-Koehler Publishers.

Boler, M. (2013). Teaching for hope: The ethics of shattering worldviews. In V. Bozalek, B. Leibowitz, R. Carolissen, & M. Boler (Eds.), *Discerning critical hope in educational practices*. London, UK: Routledge.

Boler, M., & Zembylas, M. (2003). Discomforting truths: The emotional terrain of understanding difference. In P. P. Trifonas (Ed.), *Pedagogies of difference: Rethinking education for social change* (pp. 110–136). New York and London: RoutledgeFalmer.

Booysen, L. (2007). Societal power shifts and changing social identities in South Africa: Workplace implications: management. *South African Journal of Economic and Management Sciences*, *10*(1), 1–20.

Brooks, C., & Manza, J. (1994). Do Changing Values Explain the New Politics? A Critical Assessment of the Postmaterialist Thesis. *The Sociological Quarterly*, *35*(4), 541–570. https://doi.org/10.1111/j.1533-8525.1994.tb00416.x

Bulhan, H. A. (1985). *Frantz Fanon and the Psychology of Oppression*. New York, NY & London, UK: Plenum Press.

Burger, R., & Jafta, R. (2010). Affirmative action in South Africa: An empirical assessment of the impact on labour market outcomes. *CRISE (Centre for Research on Inequality, Human Security and Ethnicity) Working Paper*, *76*, 09–36.

Butler, T., & Savage, M. (2013). *Social change and the middle classes*. Routledge.

Carton, A. M., & Rosette, A. S. (2011). Explaining Bias against Black Leaders: Integrating Theory on Information Processing and Goal-Based Stereotyping. *Academy of Management Journal*, *54*(6), 1141–1158. https://doi.org/10.5465/amj.2009.0745

Cilliers, F., & Stone, K. (2005). Employment equity practices in three South African Information Technology Organisations: A systems psychodynamic perspective. *SA Journal of Industrial Psychology*, *31*(2), 49–57.

Collins, P. H. (2000). What's Going On? Black Feminist Thought and the Politics of Postmodernism. In E. St. Pierre & W. Pillow (Eds.), *Working the Ruins: Feminist Poststructural Theory and Methods in Education* (pp. 41–73). New York, NY and London, U.K.: Routledge.

Collins, P. H. (2004). *Black sexual politics: African Americans, gender, and the new racism.* New York: Routledge.

Collins, P. H. (2009). *Black Feminist Thought.* Retrieved from https://futuresinitiative.org/para/wp-content/uploads/sites/196/2017/08/Collins-Patricia.-Black-Feminist-Thought-copy.pdf?x83816

Collins, P. H. (2015). Intersectionality's Definitional Dilemmas. *Annual Review of Sociology*, *41*(1), 1–20. https://doi.org/10.1146/annurev-soc-073014-112142

Comaroff, J., & Comaroff, J. L. (2012). *Theory from the South: Or, How Euro-America is Evolving Toward Africa.* Boulder, CO: Paradigm Publishers.

Commission for Employment Equity. (2015). *Commission for Employment Equity 15th Annual Report 2015.* Retrieved from Department of Labour website: http://www.labour.gov.za/DOL/downloads/documents/annual-reports/employment-equity/2014-2015/15th%20CEE%20Annual%20Report%202015.pdf

Commission for Employment Equity. (2016). *Commission for Employment Equity 16th Annual Report 2016.* Retrieved from Department of Labour website: http://146.141.12.21/handle/10539/20485

Commission for Employment Equity. (2017). *Commission for Employment Equity 17th Annual Report 2017* (p. 106). Retrieved from Department of Labour website: http://www.labour.gov.za/DOL/downloads/documents/annual-reports/employment-equity/2016-2017/17th%20CEE%20Annual%20Report.pdf

Congress of the People. (1955, June 26). The Freedom Charter. Retrieved 14 September 2015, from African National Congress website: http://www.anc.org.za/show.php?id=72

Crenshaw, K. W. (1989). Demarginalizing the Intersection of Race and Sex: A Black Feminist Critique of Antidiscrimination Doctrine, Feminist Theory and Antiracist Politics. *University of Chicago Legal Forum*, *1989*(1), 139–167. https://doi.org/10.12691/education-3-7-4

Crenshaw, K. W. (1991). Mapping the Margins: Intersectionality, Identity Politics, and Violence against Women of Color. *Stanford Law Review*, *43*(6), 1241. https://doi.org/10.2307/1229039

Damasio, A. (2008). *Descartes' Error: Emotion, Reason and the Human Brain.* Random House.

Davis, D., & Steyn, M. (2012). Teaching social justice: Reframing some common pedagogical assumptions. *Perspectives in Education; Bloemfontein*, *30*(4), 29-38,110-111.

Dei, G. J. S. (1999). Knowledge and Politics of Social Change: The implication of anti-racism. *British Journal of Sociology of Education*, *20*(3), 395–409. https://doi.org/10.1080/01425699995335

DeRosa, P. (2001). Social Change or Status Quo? Approaches to diversity training. *ChangeWorks Consulting*, 4.

DiAngelo, R. (2011). White Fragility. *The International Journal of Critical Pedagogy*, *3*(3). Retrieved from http://libjournal.uncg.edu/ijcp/article/view/249

DiAngelo, R. (2012). Nothing to Add—A Challenge to White Silence in Discussions of Racism. *Understanding and Dismantling Privilege*, *2*(1), 17.

Donaldson, T. (1982). *Corporations and Morality.* Englewood Cliffs, NJ: Prentice-Hall.

Donaldson, T., & Dunfee, T. W. (1999). *Ties that bind: A social contracts approach to business ethics.*

Durrheim, K., Mtose, X., & Brown, L. (2011). *Race Trouble: Race, Identity and Inequality in Post-Apartheid South Africa.* Lanham, MD: Lexington Books.

Evans, P. B., & Sewell, Jr., W. H. (2013). Neoliberalism: Policy Regimes, International Regimes, and Social Effects. In P. A. Hall & M. Lamont (Eds.), *Social Resilience in the Neoliberal Era* (pp. 35–68). New York, NY: Cambridge University Press.

Freeman, R. E. (2010). *Strategic Management: A Stakeholder Approach.* Cambridge, UK: Cambridge University Press.

Goldberg, D. T. (2001). *The Racial State.* Malden, MA: Wiley-Blackwell.

Bibliography

Gordon, L. R. (2004). Critical Reflections on Three Popular Tropes in the Study of Whiteness. In G. Yancy (Ed.), *What White Looks Like: African American Philosophers on the Whiteness Question* (pp. 173–194). Psychology Press.

Grosfoguel, R. (2009). A decolonial approach to political economy: Transmodernity, border thinking and global coloniality. *Kult, 6*, 10–38.

Gwele, N. S. (2009). Diversity management in the workplace: Beyond compliance. *Curationis, 32*(2), 4–10.

Habib, A. (2013). *South Africa's suspended revolution: Hopes and prospects*. Johannesburg: Wits University Press.

Hall, S. (1987). Minimal selves. In *ICA Documents: Vol. 6. The Real Me: Post-modernism and the question of identity* (pp. 44–46). Retrieved from http://site.ufvjm.edu.br/mpich/files/2013/04/HALL-Minimal-Selves.pdf

Hansen, F. (2003). Diversity's business case doesn't add up. *Workforce Costa Mesa, 82*(4), 28–33.

Healy, G. (2016). The Politics of Equality and Diversity: History, Society, and Biography. In *the Oxford Handbook of Diversity in Organizations* (pp. 15–39). Oxford and New York: Oxford University Press.

Hoch, J. E., Pearce, C. L., & Welzel, L. (2010). Is the most effective team leadership shared? The impact of shared leadership, age diversity, and coordination on team performance. *Journal of Personnel Psychology, 9*(3), 105–116. https://doi.org/10.1027/1866-5888/a000020

Hoffman, P. T. (2015). *Why Did Europe Conquer the World?* Princeton, NJ and Oxford, UK: Princeton University Press.

hooks, bell. (2009). *Reel to Real: Race, Sex and Class at the Movies*. New York, NY and London, UK: Routledge.

Inglehart, R. (1990). *Culture Shift in Advanced Industrial Society*. Princeton, NJ: Princeton University Press.

Inglehart, R., & Welzel, C. (2010). Changing Mass Priorities: The Link between Modernization and Democracy. *Perspectives on Politics, 8*(2), 551–567. https://doi.org/10.1017/S1537592710001258

Jack, V., & Harris, K. (2013). *Broad-based Black Economic Empowerment: The complete guide*. Northcliff: Frontrunner Publishers.

Jayne, M. E. A., & Dipboye, R. L. (2004). Leveraging diversity to improve business performance: Research findings and recommendations for organizations. *Human Resource Management, 43*(4), 409–424. https://doi.org/10.1002/hrm.20033

Johnson, A. G. (1997). *Privilege, power, and difference*. London: McGraw-Hill.

Jones, O. (2015). *The Establishment and how they get away with it*. London: Penguin Books.

Judge, M., & Nel, J. A. (2008). Exploring homophobic victimisation in Gauteng, South Africa: Issues, impacts and responses. *Cta Criminologica: Southern African Journal of Criminology, 21*(3), 19–36.

Kahane, A. (2002). Changing the world by changing how we talk and listen. *Inspiring Education (Generon)*. Retrieved from https://www.academia.edu/3223152/Changing_the_world_by_changing_how_we_talk_and_listen

Keegan, T. J. (1997). *Colonial South Africa and the Origins of the Racial Order*. London, UK: Leicester University Press.

Kelly, C., Wale, K., Soudien, C., & Steyn, M. (2007). Aligning the Diversity 'Rubik' Cube: Conceptualising Transformative Practice. *South African Journal of Labour Relations, 31*(2), 10–31.

Kelly, E., & Dobbin, F. (1998). How Affirmative Action Became Diversity Management, How Affirmative Action Became Diversity Management: Employer Response to Antidiscrimination Law, 1961 to 1996, Employer Response to Antidiscrimination Law, 1961 to 1996. *American Behavioral Scientist, 41*(7), 960–984. https://doi.org/10.1177/0002764298041007008

Kersten, A. (2000). Diversity management: Dialogue, dialectics and diversion. *Journal of Organizational Change Management, 13*(3), 235–248. https://doi.org/10.1108/09534810010330887

Khoele, A., & Daya, P. (2014). Investigating the turnover of middle and senior managers in the pharmaceutical industry in South Africa: Original research. *SA Journal of Human Resource Management, 12*(1), 1–10. https://doi.org/10.4102/sajhrm.v12i1.562

Kitch, S. (2009). *The Specter of Sex: Gendered Foundations of Racial Formation in the United States.* Albany, NY: SUNY Press.

Korn / Ferry Institute. (2007). *The cost of employee turnover due to failed diversity initiatives in the workplace: The corporate leavers survey 2007* (p. 8). Korn / Ferry Institute.

Krikler, J. (2005). *The Rand Revolt: The 1922 insurrection and racial killing in South Africa.* Johannesburg: Jonathan Ball.

Kundu, S. C. (2003). Workforce diversity status: A study of employees' reactions. *Industrial Management & Data Systems, 103*(4), 215–226. https://doi.org/10.1108/02635570310470610

Laclau, E. (1990). *New reflections on the revolution of our time.* London; New York: Verso.

Laclau, E., & Mouffe, C. (2001). *Hegemony and socialist strategy: Towards a radical democratic politics.* London; New York: Verso. (Original work published 1985)

Leonard, A. (2004). *Communicating affirmative action during transformational change: A South African case study perspective* (MPhil Dissertation, University of Pretoria). Retrieved from https://repository.up.ac.za/handle/2263/28248

Liswood, L. A. (2010). *The Loudest Duck: Moving Beyond Diversity while Embracing Differences to Achieve Success at Work.* Hoboken, NJ: John Wiley & Sons.

Litvin, D. R. (2002). The business case for diversity and the 'Iron Cage'. In B. Czarniawska & H. Höpfl (Eds.), *Casting the Other: The Production and Maintenance of Inequalities in Work Organizations* (pp. 160–184). London UK and New York NY: Routledge.

Lorde, A. (2007a). Age, Race, Class, and Sex: Women Redefining Difference. In *Sister Outsider: Essays and Speeches* (Revised, pp. 114–123). Berkeley: Crossing Press. (Original work published 1984)

Lorde, A. (2007b). *Sister Outsider: Essays and Speeches* (Revised). Berkeley: Crossing Press. (Original work published 1984)

Mamdani, M. (1997). *Citizen and Subject: Decentralized Despotism and the Legacy of Late Colonialism.* Oxford, UK: Oxford University Press.

Mangcu, X. (Ed.). (2015). *The colour of our future: Does race matter in post-apartheid South Africa?* Johannesburg: Wits University Press.

Mannheim, K. (1952). *The Problem of Generations.* London: Routledge.

@Manwhohasitall. (2018). *The Man Who Has It All: A Patronizing Parody of Self-Help Books for Women.* New York, NY: Skyhorse Publishing.

Marques, J. F. (2010). Colorful window dressing: A critical review on workplace diversity in three major American corporations. *Human Resource Development Quarterly, 21*(4), 435–446. https://doi.org/10.1002/hrdq.20045

Marx, A. W. (1998). *Making Race and Nation: A Comparison of South Africa, the United States, and Brazil.* Cambridge, UK: Cambridge University Press.

Mattes, R. (2012). The 'Born Frees': The Prospects for Generational Change in Post-apartheid South Africa. *Australian Journal of Political Science, 47*(1), 133–153. https://doi.org/10.1080/10361146.2011.643166

Mbembe, A. (2017). *Critique of Black Reason* (First; L. Dubois, Trans.). Durham, NC: Duke University Press.

McClintock, A. (1995). *Imperial leather: Race, gender, and sexuality in the colonial contest.* New York: Routledge.

McIntosh, P. (2011). White Privilege and Male Privilege: A Personal Account of Coming to See the Correspondences Through Work in Women's Studies. In E. F. Provenzo, Jr. (Ed.), *The Teacher in American Society: A Critical Anthology* (pp. 121–134). Thousand Oaks, CA and London, U.K.: SAGE. (Original work published 1988)

McIntosh, P. (2015). White Privilege: Unpacking the Invisble Knapsack. In M. Andersen & P. H. Collins (Eds.), *Race, Class, & Gender: An Anthology* (pp. 74–83). Wadsworth, Ohio: Cengage Learning. (Original work published 1989)

Milliken, F. J., & Martins, L. L. (1996). Searching for Common Threads: Understanding the Multiple Effects of Diversity in Organizational Groups. *Academy of Management Review*, *21*(2), 402–433. https://doi.org/10.5465/amr.1996.9605060217

Mills, C. W. (1997). *The racial contract*. Ithaca: Cornell University Press.

Mills, C. W. (2008). Racial liberalism. *PMLA*, 1380–1397.

Moane, G. (2003). Bridging the Personal and the Political: Practices for a Liberation Psychology. *American Journal of Community Psychology*, *31*(1–2), 91–101. https://doi.org/10.1023/A:1023026704576

Montes, T., & Shaw, G. (2003). The Future of Workplace Diversity in the New Millennium. In M. J. Davidson & S. L. Fielden (Eds.), *Individual Diversity and Psychology in Organizations* (pp. 385–402). https://doi.org/10.1002/0470013354.ch23

Motlatsi, J., & Godsell, B. (2009). *Do It!: Every South African's Guide to Making a Difference*. Johannesburg: Jacana Media.

Mtungwa, I. Q. (2009). *The black spot: A critical look at transformation in the workplace*. Create Space Independent Publishing Platform.

Narayan, U. (2013). *Dislocating Cultures: Identities, Traditions, and Third World Feminism*. New York, NY & Abingdon, UK: Routledge.

Ndebele, N. S. (2000). 'Iph' Indlela? Finding our way into the future' the first Steve Biko memorial lecture. *Social Dynamics*, *26*(1), 43–55. https://doi.org/10.1080/02533950008458685

Ndzwayiba, N. (2017) *Doing Human Differently: A Critical Analysis of Appraised Diversity Discourses in Corporate South Africa*. PhD. University of the Witwatersrand, Johannesburg

Nel, C. (2010). *Transformation without sacrifice*. Cape Town: Village of Leaders Products.

Netshitenzhe, J. (2014). Inequality matters: South African trends and interventions: socio-economic performance. *New Agenda: South African Journal of Social and Economic Policy*, *2014*(53), 8–13.

Nixon, R. (2015). *Selling Apartheid: South Africa's Global Propaganda War*. Johannesburg: Jacana Education.

Nkomo, S. (2011). Moving from the letter of the law to the spirit of the law: The challenges of realising the intent of employment equity and affirmative action. *Transformation: Critical Perspectives on Southern Africa*, *77*(1), 122–135.

Nkomo, S., & Hoobler, J. M. (2014). A historical perspective on diversity ideologies in the United States: Reflections on human resource management research and practice. *Human Resource Management Review*, *24*(3), 245–257. https://doi.org/10.1016/j.hrmr.2014.03.006

Nkomo, S. M. (1992). The Emperor Has No Clothes: Rewriting "Race in Organizations". *Academy of Management Review*, *17*(3), 487–513. https://doi.org/10.5465/AMR.1992.4281987

Nkomo, S. M. (2007). Editor's introduction to SAJLR Special Edition: Workplace diversity management: issues, controversies and practices. *South African Journal of Labour Relations: Workplace Diversity Management: Issues, Controversies and Practices: Special Issue*, *31*(2), 6–9.

Nkomo, S. M. (2014). Inclusion: Old Wine in New Bottles? In *Diversity at Work: The Practice of Inclusion* (pp. 580–592). https://doi.org/10.1002/9781118764282.ch22

Noon, M. (2007). The fatal flaws of diversity and the business case for ethnic minorities. *Work, Employment and Society*, *21*(4), 773–784. https://doi.org/10.1177/0950017007082886

Norval, A. J. (1996). *Deconstructing apartheid discourse*. New York: Verso.

Nzukuma, K. C. C., & Bussin, M. (2011). Job-hopping amongst African Black senior management in South Africa: Original research. *SA Journal of Human Resource Management*, *9*(1), 1–12.

Parker, M. (2001). Fucking Management: Queer, Theory and Reflexivity. *Ephemera: Critical Dialogues on Organization*, *1*(1), 36–53.

Payne, D. A. R., & Thakkar, D. B. S. (2012). The Hypocrisy of Affirmative Action: Race and The Labor Market. *Far East Journal of Psychology and Business*, *9 No 1 Paper 1 October* (1), 1–14.

Pelled, L. H. (1996). Demographic Diversity, Conflict, and Work Group Outcomes: An Intervening Process Theory. *Organization Science*, *7*(6), 615–631. https://doi.org/10.1287/orsc.7.6.615

Peyper, L. (2016, July 18). Black professionals earn significantly less than whites. *CityPress*. Retrieved from https://city-press.news24.com/Business/black-professionals-earn-significantly-less-than-whites-20160718

Pheterson, G. (1986). Alliances between Women: Overcoming Internalized Oppression and Internalized Domination. *Signs: Journal of Women in Culture and Society, 12*(1), 146–160. https://doi.org/10.1086/494302

Piketty, T. (2014). *Capital in the twenty-first century* (First). Cambridge, MA: The Belknap Press of Harvard University Press.

Pioneers of Change Associates. (2006). *Mapping Dialogue: A research project profiling dialogue tools and processes* (p. 85). Retrieved from GTZ website: http://www.mspguide.org/sites/default/files/resource/mapping_dialogue_-_a_research_project_profiling_dialogue_tools_and_processes.pdf

Posel, D. (2010). Races to consume: Revisiting South Africa's history of race, consumption and the struggle for freedom. *Ethnic & Racial Studies, 33*(2), 157–175. https://doi.org/10.1080/01419870903428505

Pothier, D., & Devlin, R. (2006). *Critical Disability Theory: Essays in Philosophy, Politics, Policy, and Law*. Vancouver and Toronto: UBC Press.

Roberson, Q. M. (2006). Disentangling the Meanings of Diversity and Inclusion in Organizations. *Group & Organization Management, 31*(2), 212–236.

Roberson, Q. M., & Stevens, C. K. (2006). Making sense of diversity in the workplace: Organizational justice and language abstraction in employees' accounts of diversity-related incidents. *Journal of Applied Psychology, 91*(2), 379–391. https://doi.org/10.1037/0021-9010.91.2.379

Ryder, N. (1965). The Cohort as a Concept in the Study of Social Change. *American Sociological Review, 30*(6), 843–861. https://doi.org/10.2307/2090964

Selby, K., & Sutherland, M. (2006). "Space creation": A strategy for achieving employment equity at senior management level. *South African Journal of Labour Relations, 30*(2), 42–65.

Sethi, S. P. (1975). Dimensions of Corporate Social Performance: An Analytical Framework, Dimensions of Corporate Social Performance: An Analytical Framework. *California Management Review, 17*(3), 58–64. https://doi.org/10.2307/41162149

Singleton, G. E., & Linton, C. (2007). *Courageous conversations about race: A field guide for achieving equity in schools*. Thousand Oaks, CA: Corwin Press.

Solnit, R. (2012, August 20). Men Explain Things to Me. Retrieved 16 October 2018, from Mag website: https://www.guernicamag.com/rebecca-solnit-men-explain-things-to-me/

Sonn, M., & Batts, V. (1985). Strategies for Changing Personal Attitudes of White Racism. *Papers Delivered at the Annual Convention of the American Psychological Association*. Presented at the Annual Convention of the American Psychological Association, Los Angeles, CA.

Statistics South Africa, & Lehohla, P. (Eds.). (2014). *Census 2011: Profile of persons with disabilities in South Africa*. Pretoria: Statistics South Africa.

Steyn, M. E. (2001). Whiteness in the Rainbow: Experiencing the Loss of Privilege in the New South Africa. In C. V. Hamilton, L. Huntley, N. Alexander, A. S. A. Guimarães, & W. James (Eds.), *Beyond Racism: Race and Inequality in Brazil, South Africa, and the United States* (pp. 85–104). Boulder, CO and London, UK: Lynne Rienner Publishers.

Steyn, M. E. (Ed.). (2010). *Being Different Together: Case Studies on Diversity Interventions in some South African Organisations*. Retrieved from http://localhost:8080/handle/123456789/107

Steyn, M. E. (2015). Critical Diversity LIteracy. In *Routledge International Handbook of Diversity Studies* (pp. 379–389). Abingdon and New York: Routledge.

Steyn, M. E., Burnett, S., & Ndzwayiba, N. A. (Forthcoming). Mapping capacity to deal with difference: Towards a diagnostic tool for Critical Diversity Literacy (CDL). *African Journal of Employee Relations*.

Tauss, A. (2017). Contextualizing the Current Crisis: Post-fordism, Neoliberal Restructuring, and Financialization. *Colombia Internacional*. Retrieved from https://revistas.uniandes.edu.co/doi/abs/10.7440/colombiaint76.2012.03

Taylor, S. D. (2007). *Business and the State in Southern Africa: The Politics of Economic Reform*. Boulder, CO: Lynne Rienner.

Thomas, R. R. (1990). From affirmative action to affirming diversity. *Harvard Business Review, 68*(2), 107–117.

Bibliography

Tilley, J. R. (2005). Research Note: Libertarian-Authoritarian Value Change in Britain, 1974–2001, Research Note: Libertarian-Authoritarian Value Change in Britain, 1974–2001. *Political Studies, 53*(2), 442–453. https://doi.org/10.1111/j.1467-9248.2005.00537.x

Tlou, B. L., & Schurink, W. (2003). A gay woman's experiences during her career in the Department of Defence: Fleet of hope. *SA Journal of Human Resource Management, 1*(3), 24–34.

Twine, F. W. (2010). *A White Side of Black Britain: Interracial Intimacy and Racial Literacy*. Durham, NC and London, UK: Duke University Press.

Ulrich, N. (2016). Rethinking Citizenship and Subjecthood in South Africa: Khoesan, Labor Relations, and the Colonial State in the Cape of Good Hope (c. 1652-1815). In E. Hunter (Ed.), *Citizenship, Belonging, and Political Community in Africa: Dialogues between Past and Present*. Athens, OH: Ohio University Press.

Vertovec, S. (2012). "Diversity" and the Social Imaginary. *European Journal of Sociology / Archives Européennes de Sociologie, 53*(3), 287–312. https://doi.org/10.1017/S000397561200015X

Visser, W. (2007). A racially divided class: Strikes in South Africa, 1973-2004. In S. van der Velden, H. Dribbusch, D. Lyddon, & K. Vandaele (Eds.), *Strikes Around the World, 1968-2005: Case-studies of 15 countries* (pp. 40–60). Amsterdam: Aksant Academic Publishers.

Wilkinson, K. (2016, April 19). Mail Online's claim of 400,000+ poor whites in South Africa incorrect [Fact Checking]. Retrieved 1 November 2017, from Africa Check website: https://africacheck.org/reports/mail-onlines-claim-of-400000-poor-whites-in-south-africa-incorrect/

Wilkinson, K. (2017, May 8). FACTSHEET: Statistics on farm attacks and murders in South Africa. Retrieved 16 October 2018, from Africa Check website: https://africacheck.org/factsheets/factsheet-statistics-farm-attacks-murders-sa/

Wilkinson, R., & Pickett, K. (2009). *The spirit level: Why more equal societies almost always do better*. London: Allen Lane.

Worden, N. (2012). *The making of modern South Africa: Conquest, apartheid, democracy* (5th ed.). Malden, MA and Oxford, UK: John Wiley & Sons.

Young, I. M. (2000). Five faces of oppression. In M. Adams, W. J. Blumenfeld, R. Castañeda, H. W. Hackman, M. L. Peters, & X. Zúñiga (Eds.), *Readings for diversity and social justice* (pp. 35–49). New York: Routledge.

Yuval-Davis, N. (2006a). Belonging and the politics of belonging. *Patterns of Prejudice, 40*(3), 197–214. https://doi.org/10.1080/00313220600769331

Yuval-Davis, N. (2006b). Intersectionality and Feminist Politics. *European Journal of Women's Studies, 13*(3), 193–209. https://doi.org/10.1177/1350506806065752

www.ingramcontent.com/pod-product-compliance
Lightning Source LLC
Chambersburg PA
CBHW052011030426
42334CB00029BA/3180